EDITED BY
JESSICA JACOBSON AND
PENNY COOPER

PARTICIPATION
IN COURTS AND
TRIBUNALS

Concepts, Realities and Aspirations

Foreword by the Rt Hon Sir Ernest Ryder

BRISTOL
UNIVERSITY
PRESS

T0366522

First published in Great Britain in 2020 by

Bristol University Press
University of Bristol
1-9 Old Park Hill
Bristol
BS2 8BB
UK
t: +44 (0)117 954 5940
e: bup-info@bristol.ac.uk

Details of international sales and distribution partners are available at bristoluniversitypress.co.uk

© Bristol University Press 2020

British Library Cataloguing in Publication Data

A catalogue record for this book is available from the British Library

ISBN 978-1-5292-1129-0 hardcover
ISBN 978-1-5292-1146-7 paperback (NOT FOR GENERAL SALE)
ISBN 978-1-5292-1131-3 ePub
ISBN 978-1-5292-1130-6 OA ePdf

Cover design by blu inc, Bristol
Cover image credit: macu-ic-PbN_Gl_ZoMk-unsplash
Printed and bound in Great Britain by CPI Group (UK) Ltd, Croydon, CR0 4YY
Bristol University Press uses environmentally responsible print partners.

Contents

List of Boxes, Figures and Tables

Notes on Contributors

Penny Cooper is Visiting Professor at the School of Law at Birkbeck, University of London, and Senior Research Fellow at Birkbeck's Institute for Crime & Justice Policy Research (ICPR). She has held professorial posts at three other universities in London and was an Associate Dean at the law school at City, University of London until 2012. She co-founded and chairs the leading website 'The Advocate's Gateway', created ground rules hearings and devised the English witness intermediary model. She is co-editor of the leading text *Vulnerable People and the Criminal Justice System*, published by Oxford University Press in 2017. Penny has been a barrister since 1990, is based at 39 Essex Chambers, London and specialises in witness preparation for commercial cases.

Gillian Hunter is Senior Research Fellow at ICPR. Prior to joining ICPR in 2003, she worked on health-based social research at the Centre for Drugs and Health Behaviour, then based at Imperial College, London. Her current research interests focus on access to justice and victims', witnesses' and defendants' experiences of the criminal justice system. Her publications include *Inside Crown Court: Personal Experiences and Questions of Legitimacy* (Policy Press, 2015, with Jessica Jacobson and Amy Kirby). She has also recently conducted research on problem-solving approaches in the Youth Court and evidence-based practice in policing and crime reduction.

Jessica Jacobson is Director of ICPR and Professor of Criminal Justice at Birkbeck. She was formerly a researcher in the Home Office and also worked for many years as an independent policy researcher and consultant. She undertakes research and publishes on many aspects of the justice system, including prisons, sentencing and the work of the courts more widely. Her recent publications include *Inside Crown Court: Personal Experiences and Questions of Legitimacy* (Policy Press, 2015, with Gillian Hunter and Amy Kirby) and *Imprisonment Worldwide: The Current Situation and an Alternative Future* (Policy Press, 2016, with Andrew Coyle, Helen Fair and Roy Walmsley).

Amy Kirby is Lecturer in the Department of Criminology at Birkbeck. She was awarded a PhD from the University of Surrey in 2019 for her study of lay participants' perceptions of the legitimacy of the criminal courts, funded by the Economic and Social Research Council. Over the last decade, her research and teaching has focused on a range of criminal justice oriented topics, including: the criminal courts and sentencing, 'court culture', legitimacy, victimology, youth justice and joint enterprise. She is co-author of *Inside Crown Court: Personal Experiences and Questions of Legitimacy* (Policy Press, 2015, with Jessica Jacobson and Gillian Hunter).

Acknowledgements

This book is the culmination of an ambitious, wide-ranging research project, to which a great many people contributed. We would like to express our sincere gratitude to all the individuals across our research sites who took time out of busy work schedules to assist with the research by offering practical support and taking part in research interviews. We are grateful also to Dr Bina Bhardwa, Helen Fair and Dr Emily Setty who were part of the research team which conducted the interviews and court observations; and also to Emily Setty for her contribution to the policy review conducted as part of the study.

We received invaluable advice and guidance from a judicial reference group and project steering group. For their insightful comments on drafts of this volume, we would especially like to thank Dr Bina Bhardwa, Professor Mike Hough, Dr Camillia Kong, Professor Grainne McKeever, Alex Ruck Keen, Jenny Talbot, David Wurtzel, the anonymous Bristol University Press reviewer and several members of the judiciary.

For their approval of and assistance with research access, we wish to thank the Judicial Office, the Ministry of Justice National Research Committee, the HMCTS Data Access Panel, Cafcass, Cafcass Cymru, the Citizens Advice Witness Service and the Personal Support Unit (now Support Through Court). We are also grateful to the Commission on Justice in Wales, and particularly its Chair Lord Thomas of Cwmgiedd and Secretary Andrew Felton, for their support and help with access to relevant services and individuals in the research site in Wales.

Thanks are also due to the following individuals who facilitated Penny Cooper's visits and supported research about jurisdictions outside England and Wales, findings from which are reported in Chapter Five: Tim Barraclough, Angelica Blasi, Laura Cilesio, Kristy Crepaldi, Professor Coral Dando, Sheriff Alistair Duff, Elron Elahie, Adrienne Finney, Judge Jennie Girdham, Veronica Holland, Justice Iain Morley, Carolina Puyol, Dr Liz Spruin, Justice V. Georgis Taylor-Alexander, Heidi Yates and colleagues at ACT Human Rights Commission and DCI Peter Yeomans.

This project was generously funded by the Nuffield Foundation. The Nuffield Foundation is an independent charitable trust with a mission to advance social well-being. It funds research that informs social policy, primarily in education, welfare, and justice. It also funds student programmes that provide opportunities for young people to develop skills in quantitative and scientific methods. The Nuffield Foundation is the founder and co-funder of the Nuffield Council on Bioethics and the Ada Lovelace Institute. The Foundation has funded this project, but the views expressed are those of the authors and not necessarily the Foundation. Visit www.nuffieldfoundation.org.

Foreword

I am delighted to introduce the findings of this major research project funded by the Nuffield Foundation. I am very grateful to Jessica Jacobson, Penny Cooper, Gillian Hunter and Amy Kirby for the quality of the work that has been undertaken and for the collaboration that this has involved between the academy, the judiciary and those representing courts and tribunals users.

The authors' central thesis is that people should be able to participate effectively in the court and tribunal proceedings that directly concern them. The project involved 159 interviews with judges, lawyers, court staff and other practitioners and over 300 hours' observational research conducted in criminal and family courts and employment and immigration and asylum tribunals. The study shows that practitioners do, by and large, make sincere efforts to help lay users participate in proceedings; yet many barriers to participation remain which can leave users marginalised in hearings. It is the responsibility of all those who work in courts and tribunals to understand these barriers and take steps to help users overcome them – this study provides insight and practical suggestions.

The researchers are correct to call on policy makers, judges and other practitioners to use and further elaborate on the *Ten Points of Participation* that have emerged from this study. The researchers also make the case for international collaboration and much-needed research with users themselves. As discussed in the final chapter, the findings of this study not only have relevance to the way we conduct face-to-face hearings, but also to COVID-19 remote hearings and future plans for the use of technology in courts and tribunals.

The researchers have studied national and international court and tribunal practice in a way never done before. This accessible, timely and important volume and the policy briefing and practitioner toolkit being published alongside it will help place users at the heart of court and tribunal reform. I commend this volume to all those who work in courts and tribunals and everyone interested in how users participate in hearings.

Rt Hon Sir Ernest Ryder, Senior President of Tribunals

ONE

Introduction

Jessica Jacobson

Key messages of this volume

It is a long-established legal principle in England and Wales – expressed in statute, case law, procedure rules, practice directions and guidance – that people should be able to *participate effectively* in the court and tribunal proceedings that directly concern them. There is wide agreement among law reformers and commentators, as well as among the judiciary and legal practitioners, that participation is essential to the delivery of justice.

But what exactly does it mean for a lay person to participate effectively in judicial proceedings – whether the individual is a defendant or complainant in a criminal case, a party in a family dispute, a claimant or respondent in the Employment Tribunal, an appellant against an immigration or asylum decision, or a witness in any such setting? Why does their participation matter? What factors typically impede their participation and how can it be better supported? This book addresses these pressing, but hitherto neglected, questions in reporting on a unique study which combined cross-jurisdictional socio-legal policy analysis with close empirical inquiry.

A raft of policy initiatives over the past two decades have sought to bolster participation in judicial proceedings, and particularly that of individuals considered 'vulnerable'. Other developments in law and policy have, conversely, undermined the scope or capacity of court users to participate. These include reduced availability of publicly funded legal representation, and wide-scale court closures and the accompanying growing dependence on remote participation through live video- or audio-link and online processes. At the time this book is being completed (May 2020), the existing trend towards replacement of physical with virtual court attendance has accelerated to an extent few could have foreseen – as a result of the COVID-19 pandemic and the imperative to maintain social distancing within the justice system, as across all parts of society.[1] While it is as yet too early to assess the long-term implications for judicial proceedings of changes arising from the public health emergency, these developments make all the more urgent the need to consider what 'participation' means, why it matters and what can be done to ensure it is genuinely effective.

Judges, lawyers, court staff and other practitioners interviewed for this study – from the criminal and family courts and employment and immigration and asylum tribunals – made clear their commitment to the principle of effective participation. They spoke of participation not simply as an abstract concept, but as something that they actively mediated and facilitated, in their differing professional capacities. Courtroom observations conducted by the research team confirmed that practitioners do, by and large, make sincere efforts to help court users to participate; and that, moreover, they treat court users with courtesy, respect and kindness. And yet the observations also shed light on the profound limits to participation by individuals whose powerlessness and disadvantages are laid bare in the courtroom.

The findings of this study point to not only the facilitators of and barriers to participation, but also its multifaceted nature. It was defined in a wide range of ways by the interviewed practitioners. Across the range of court and tribunal settings, participation was variously said to be a matter of providing and eliciting information for the court; being informed; being legally represented; being protected; being managed; and being present. Its functions were described in terms of the exercise of legal rights; enabling court decision making; legitimation of court processes and outcomes; and potential therapeutic benefits.

If policy and practice are to better support participation in the future, especially at times of rapid change to the wider policy landscape, there must be a clear understanding and articulation of its many different aspects and the interplay between them. It should be recognised that all aspects are pertinent – potentially at least – to any setting, and that an over-emphasis on some at the cost of others risks undermining participation and further marginalising the individual court user. This book calls on legal professionals and practitioners, as well as policy makers and other researchers, to apply the framework for understanding participation that is set out here, and to elaborate it further as needed. We also intend the framework to be used to open up discussions with court users themselves about what they expect of judicial proceedings and what is expected of them.

Investigating participation

Despite the significance of effective participation as a principle in English law, the concept has to date been subject to little critical analysis or empirical investigation. This volume presents the findings of a wide-ranging study, funded by the Nuffield Foundation, of participation in judicial proceedings. The research was conducted by a team based at the Institute for Crime and Justice Policy Research (ICPR) at Birkbeck, University of London, comprising the contributors to this volume (Penny Cooper, Gillian Hunter, Jessica Jacobson and Amy Kirby) and three other researchers: Bina Bhardwa, Helen Fair and Emily Setty.

The study combined a national and international policy review with extensive empirical research in a range of court and tribunal settings in England and Wales. The following questions were addressed:

- What does it mean, in both theory and practice, for lay court and tribunal users to participate effectively in court and tribunal proceedings?
- Why does participation matter?
- What factors (procedural, environmental, social, personal) impede and, conversely, facilitate participation by lay court and tribunal users – including those who are and those who are not legally represented?
- What are the implications for participation of ongoing policy developments, including cuts to legal aid and the court reform programme being implemented by HM Courts and Tribunals Service (HMCTS)?
- How might policy and practice better support participation in the future?

Study parameters

The parameters of the study were broad. The research explored the scope and nature of participation by lay people attending oral hearings across different judicial settings – primarily, in the criminal and family courts and employment and immigration and asylum tribunals – and in different capacities: see Box 1.1. The usefulness of a generic, cross-jurisdictional approach to participation was thus a central consideration in the research.

Box 1.1: Definitions

Lay court and tribunal users include:

- **witnesses** called to give oral evidence to the court or tribunal (*excluding* expert witnesses – that is, those giving opinion evidence based on specialist knowledge);

- **parties** to oral hearings in the court or tribunal – specifically:
    - defendants in criminal cases in the Crown and magistrates' courts;
    - parties (primarily parents) in Family Court hearings;
    - claimants and respondents in Employment Tribunal hearings;
    - appellants in hearings of the First-tier Tribunal (Immigration and Asylum Chamber).

In this volume, the term '**court users**' is used as a shorthand for lay court and tribunal users; and the term '**courts**' is used as a shorthand for courts and tribunals.

Within the criminal jurisdiction, the research encompassed adult magistrates' courts, where all criminal proceedings start and most are dealt with in their entirety; and the Crown Court, which tries and sentences serious cases and hears appeals from magistrates' courts. The Family Court[2] deals with a wide variety of matters relating to families; here, the study's main focus was on Children Act cases[3] – both public law (concerning local authority applications for orders to safeguard children's welfare) and private law (concerning applications for child arrangements orders by private individuals). The Employment Tribunal (ET) hears claims against employers about such matters as unfair dismissal or discrimination; while the First-tier Tribunal (Immigration and Asylum Chamber) (IAC) handles appeals against Home Office decisions, and has UK-wide jurisdiction. These courts and tribunals make up a substantial part of the justice system in England and Wales, as made

PARTICIPATION IN COURTS AND TRIBUNALS

Figure 1.1: Major first-instance courts and tribunals in England and Wales

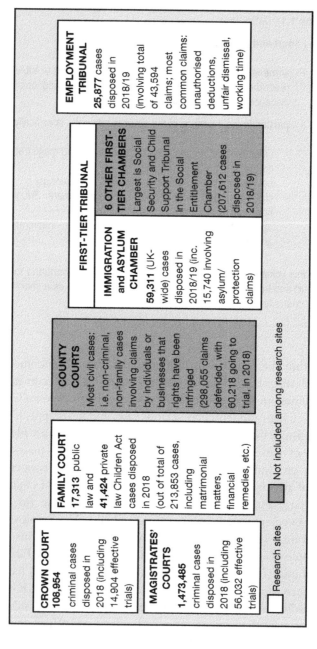

CROWN COURT
108,954 criminal cases disposed in 2018 (including 14,904 effective trials)

MAGISTRATES' COURTS
1,473,485 criminal cases disposed in 2018 (including 56,032 effective trials)

FAMILY COURT
17,313 public law and **41,424** private law Children Act cases disposed in 2018 (out of total of 213,853 cases, including matrimonial matters, financial remedies, etc.)

COUNTY COURTS
Most civil cases; i.e. non-criminal, non-family cases involving claims by individuals or businesses that rights have been infringed (298,055 claims defended, with 60,218 going to trial, in 2018)

FIRST-TIER TRIBUNAL

IMMIGRATION and ASYLUM CHAMBER
59,311 (UK-wide) cases disposed in 2018/19 (inc. 15,740 involving asylum/protection claims)

6 OTHER FIRST-TIER CHAMBERS
Largest is Social Security and Child Support Tribunal in the Social Entitlement Chamber (207,612 cases disposed in 2018/19)

EMPLOYMENT TRIBUNAL
25,877 cases disposed in 2018/19 (involving total of 43,594 claims; most common claims: unauthorised deductions, unfair dismissal, working time)

☐ Research sites   ▨ Not included among research sites

Source: Ministry of Justice (2019)[5]

6

clear by Figure 1.1. They are settings in which, every week, many thousands of legal decisions are made with potentially far-reaching consequences for ordinary people's lives.[4]

The decision to focus the research on the courts and tribunals named earlier reflected not only their reach and significance, but also – given the research team's interest in 'participation' in the broadest sense – their diversity in terms of types of disputes adjudicated, levels of formality of proceedings, extent of self-representation of parties and history of provision for vulnerable court users. This diversity, moreover, means that the research findings are likely to have applicability to other types of court and tribunal; as suggested also by the emergence of common themes from across the justice system in the policy and academic literature reviewed for this study. The selection of research sites was also informed by the advice of a project steering group and judicial reference group and practical considerations such as ease of research access.

'Vulnerability' and 'participation'

As will be discussed later and in subsequent chapters of this volume, much of the existing law and policy around participation in courts and tribunals has tended to address the issue through the prism of court user vulnerability. That is, the focus has been on how the minority of court users identified as vulnerable – usually understood to be on the basis that they are a child or that they are an adult with a 'disorder', 'impairment' or 'disability' – can be helped to participate in proceedings. Reflecting this, the present study was originally conceived as an examination of provision for vulnerable court users. However, as the work got under way, the research team became increasingly aware of the problematic aspects of the concept of vulnerability in the context of judicial proceedings. It is apparent that a vast array of personal and social attributes, many of which are not readily identifiable, can potentially hinder a court user's capacity to understand or engage fully with the court process. Further, many intrinsic features of the court process itself can add to an individual's 'vulnerability' and further impede participation.[6] The research team consequently decided that what was of greatest interest to them was the nature of, limits to and potential supports for *participation by all court users*, rather than the question of how court users deemed vulnerable could be better provided for.

'Participation' in law and legal procedure

In criminal law, there has long been a recognition that defendants should be able to participate effectively in order to exercise their right to a fair trial under Article 6 of the European Convention on Human Rights (ECHR). 'Minimum rights' of the criminally accused under Article 6.3 comprise: (a) being promptly informed 'in a language which he understands and in detail' about the charge; (b) having 'adequate time and facilities' to prepare the defence; (c) 'to defend himself in person or through legal assistance of his own choosing'; (d) 'to examine or have examined witnesses against him', as well as 'witnesses on his behalf'; and (e) to have access to interpretation if needed. European Court of Human Rights guidance (2019: 27) stipulates that Article 6 'guarantees the right of an accused to participate effectively in a criminal trial ... In general this includes, inter alia, not only his or her right to be present, but also to hear and follow the proceedings.' Among the most significant case law supporting this principle is *SC* v *UK* ([2005] 40 EHRR 10), in which the European Court of Human Rights ruled that an 11-year-old's right to a fair trial had been breached because he had had insufficient understanding of proceedings and their consequences. According to Owusu-Bempah (2018), however, there has been little legal scrutiny of the concept of defendants' effective participation since *SC* v *UK*, other than through the Law Commission's review of fitness to plead

(2016).[7] The criteria for determining fitness to plead (although criticised by the Law Commission for being out of date and inconsistently applied) support the principle of effective participation; they are generally understood in terms of capacity to understand the charge(s), decide on plea, challenge jurors, instruct a lawyer, follow proceedings and give evidence (Law Commission, 2016: 10–11).

Fair trial rights are applicable to civil as well as criminal trials,[8] but are not generally understood to extend to complainants and other witnesses in criminal cases (other than in relation to any civil law claims they might make arising out of the crime) (von Wistinghausen, 2013; Fundamental Rights Agency, 2016). Thus, support in law for witnesses' participation is largely framed in terms other than the right to a fair trial – most commonly, with reference to the need to improve the quality of witnesses' evidence. This, for example, is the main expressed aim of the 'special measures' provisions of Part II of the Youth Justice and Criminal Evidence Act 1999, whereby witnesses (but not the accused) identified as vulnerable can give evidence from behind a screen, by live video-link, with assistance from an intermediary, or with other specified forms of help. The Criminal Procedure Rules 2015 set a broader goal, in requiring the courts 'to facilitate the participation of *any person, including the defendant*' (para 3.9.(3)(b), emphasis added).[9] To this end, the Criminal Practice Directions (3D: 'Vulnerable people in the courts') require courts 'to take "every reasonable step"'.[10] These provisions thus treat witnesses and defendants – and particularly those who are vulnerable – as entitled to help to participate in proceedings, but do not elaborate on the concept of participation or reference 'effectiveness'.

In terms that are similarly generic and again link the issue to that of vulnerability, participation is emphasised by the Family Procedure Rules. Part 3A (effective from 27 November 2017) is titled 'Vulnerable persons: participation in proceedings and giving evidence', and sets out the circumstances in which a court should make a 'participation direction', which is analogous to a special measures direction in the criminal courts.[11] This provision is supplemented by Family Practice Direction 3AA, which (para 3.1) directs courts to:

consider the ability of the party or witness to –
a) understand the proceedings, and their role in them, when in court;
b) put their views to the court;
c) instruct their representative/s before, during and after the hearing; and
d) attend the hearing without significant distress.[12]

As observed by McKeever (2020), a defining feature of the 'normative model' of tribunal hearings – especially since the creation of HMCTS in 2011 merged tribunals with courts in a single service – is that litigants should be better able to participate without representation than they are in the courts. While she questions the extent to which this model is realised in practice, the aspiration to facilitate participation is, in some respects, embedded in tribunal structures and procedures that are overall less legalistic and adversarial and more informal than those of the (civil and criminal) courts. The IAC Procedure Rules state that cases should be dealt with 'fairly and justly', which is said to include 'avoiding unnecessary formality and seeking flexibility in the proceedings' and 'ensuring, so far as practicable, that the parties are able to participate fully in the proceedings' (para 2(2)(b) and (c)).[13] The ET Procedure Rules include a similar direction to that in the IAC Rules to 'deal with cases fairly and justly', including by reducing formality and seeking flexibility (para 2(b) and (c)); here, however, 'participation' is not explicitly mentioned.[14]

The *Equal Treatment Bench Book*, published by the Judicial College (2018), provides guidance to judges and magistrates working across the courts and tribunals system. Its stated purpose is 'to increase awareness and understanding of the different circumstances of people appearing in courts and tribunals. It helps enable effective communication and suggests steps which should increase participation by all parties'.[15] The guidance stresses the centrality of participation to the fair and just operation of the courts; noting in the introduction, for example, that: 'Effective communication underlies the entire legal process: ensuring that everyone involved understands and is understood. Otherwise the legal process will be impeded or derailed' (2018: 4). Included in the guidance are 'practical suggestions … for enabling LIPs [litigants-in-person] to participate fully in the court process' (2018: 10); and consideration of the adaptations expected of courts and tribunals 'to facilitate the effective participation of witnesses, defendants and litigants' who are children or vulnerable adults (2018: 48).

In the legal, procedural and guidance documentation reviewed very briefly earlier, a variety of terminology is used: references to 'participation' in general, to 'effective participation', to help for court users to 'participate fully' and to 'effective communication'. It is clear that participation is widely treated as 'a core element of procedural and substantive justice and of legal values embedded in procedural rules' (McKeever, 2020). It is, moreover, deemed to be closely interrelated to the broader principle of access to justice. For example, Article 13.1 of the UN Convention on the Rights of Persons with Disabilities (UNCRPD), to which the UK has been a signatory since 2007, requires that persons with disabilities should have 'effective access to justice … on an equal basis with others … *in order to facilitate their effective role as direct and indirect participants*' (emphasis added).[16] The research reported on in this volume aims to provide insight into whether and in what ways participation does indeed contribute to the delivery of justice, and its constraints and limitations.

The study

This study comprised two main components: a review of national and international policy pertinent to the theme of participation, and an empirical investigation of practice. The study findings and conclusions are presented over the four chapters of this volume following this introduction.

Chapter Two, by Gillian Hunter, discusses the key policy and practice reforms in England and Wales over the past 20 years and their implications – both positive and negative – for participation by lay people in judicial proceedings. Through a narrative review of research and policy literature, and reflecting some current debates about access to justice, the national policy review sets the context for subsequent chapters. It provides a brief chronology of the introduction of various special measures for supporting court users and examines how professional practice is changing in response to guidance and advice about how lay participation can be better facilitated. It explores what existing research tells us about court users' experiences of judicial proceedings, including the barriers they have faced in understanding and engaging with the judicial process. The chapter also reflects on the (potential) effects on court users of the government's ongoing courts modernisation programme and the significantly reduced availability of publicly funded legal representation. Additionally, in light of the extraordinary circumstances that prevail as this volume is being completed, some questions are posed about supporting lay participation in the courts at a time of pandemic lockdown.

Chapters Three and Four are concerned with the empirical component of the study. There were two parts to this empirical investigation, both of which were qualitative: interviews with practitioners working in and around the courts, the findings of which are presented by Amy Kirby in Chapter Three; and observations of court hearings, as described by Jessica Jacobson in Chapter Four. Both the interviews and the observations were conducted by the team of seven researchers in three cities of roughly comparable size located in Wales and two regions of England. (Where needed in order to access a sufficient number of court and tribunal hearing centres, the fieldwork extended to neighbouring areas of the cities.) Formal approval for the research was obtained by HMCTS and the Judicial Office, as well as other relevant bodies at national and local levels.[17] Further information on methodology is provided at the outset of each chapter.

The purpose of the practitioner interviews was to explore respondents' views, based on their professional experience, of the meaning of 'participation' by court users, whether and why it is important, and the factors that support and impede it. A total of 159 practitioners were interviewed, mostly one-to-one, but occasionally in small groups; they included members of the judiciary, lawyers, court staff and others. The large majority of practitioners worked predominantly or solely in the field of criminal, family, employment or immigration law, while a small number worked in other parts of the justice system, including the coronial jurisdiction, where issues of participation are pertinent.[18] As described in Chapter Three, the interview data revealed contrasting but overlapping conceptualisations among practitioners of what participation *entails*: they spoke of it as a matter of informing and eliciting information; being informed; being represented in court; being protected; being managed; and, in its weakest sense, being present. Practitioners variously explained the *importance* of participation in terms of: the exercise of legal rights; the essential part it plays in court decision making; its legitimating function; and a possible therapeutic value for court users.

The observational research was carried out with the aim of exploring how, in practice, court users participate in hearings. The research team conducted the observations over the course of 90 visits to 17 venues – spending a total of 316 hours across all the (criminal and family) court and (ET and IAC) tribunal settings. It is argued in Chapter Four that while the settings differed widely from one another, there were also many commonalities across them. Almost every case that was observed had at its heart a story of conflict, loss and disadvantage; and each court user's 'participation' in the case could be understood as a process by which they told, or had told on their behalf, their own version of that story. Practitioners in the courtroom – including judges, magistrates, lawyers, legal advisors and others – made extensive efforts to help court users to participate, and tended to treat them respectfully and sympathetically. At the same time, it was evident that the very nature of the court process, which involved the translation of court users' stories into legal questions and legal answers, was marginalising and disempowering.

The empirical data presented in Chapters Three and Four are fully anonymised: no details that could identify any of respondents or observed cases are included. Since the findings did not point to any major differences between the three sites in terms of approaches to participation, the material is presented collectively rather than by area. It is not claimed that the interview responses and observational data are representative of courts and tribunals across England and Wales. However, the breadth of the work (in terms of its jurisdictional reach and numbers of interviews and observations conducted) and its depth (arising from the qualitative approach, which involved close examination of practitioners' views and day-to-day court proceedings) provides for a unique and compelling dataset, especially when considered in the context of the wider policy analysis.

Chapter Five, by Penny Cooper, concludes the volume by making the case for a principled approach to supporting participation across the justice system. In so doing, Cooper discusses what such an approach would entail; considers what can be learnt about supporting participation from other jurisdictions and what other jurisdictions have learnt from England and Wales; and reflects on how learning can best be shared, in both national and international settings.

These issues are considered in light of current responses to the COVID-19 pandemic, which has already provided a major impetus – in England and Wales and across much of the globe – to rapidly expanded use of alternatives to face-to-face court attendance and hearings. Cooper argues that while these current developments are urgent and largely ad hoc responses to an unprecedented public health emergency, and the extent to which they will lead to sustained change is not yet known, they compel us to think in innovative and creative ways about the fundamental nature and purpose of oral hearings in the justice system.

Cooper also observes that the complex theme of lay court users' participation in judicial proceedings, and the policy goal of better supporting participation, demands further research – including research which solicits court users' accounts of their own expectations and experiences, and further international studies. She also explores how the findings of this study could, in a very immediate and practical way, enhance practitioners' and policy makers' engagement with court users.

Notes

1   Sections 53–57 of the Coronavirus Act 2020 expanded the availability of live video and audio links in courts and tribunals.
2   The unified Family Court was created by the Crime and Courts Act 2013, and came into being in April 2014. It hears with almost all family proceedings in England and Wales, and its judiciary includes High Court judges, circuit judges, district judges and magistrates, sitting in a range of court settings.
3   That is, proceedings under the Children Act 1989.
4   It should be noted that Figure 1.1 does not provide a full picture of cases culminating in oral hearings in each jurisdiction, as comprehensive information on this is lacking.
5   *Criminal Court Statistics Quarterly: July to September 2019* (Tables M1, M2, C1, C2), www.gov.uk/government/statistics/criminal-court-statistics-quarterly-july-to-september-2019; *Family Court Statistics Quarterly: July to September 2019* (Table 1), www.gov.uk/government/statistics/family-court-statistics-quarterly-july-to-september-2019; *Civil Justice Statistics Quarterly: July to September 2019* (Table 1.1), www.gov.uk/government/statistics/civil-justice-statistics-quarterly-july-to-september-2019; *Tribunal Statistics Quarterly: July to September 2019* (Tables S1, FIA_2, ET_2, ET_3), www.gov.uk/government/statistics/tribunal-statistics-quarterly-july-to-september-2019
6   There are growing critiques of the concept of 'vulnerability' within other spheres of public policy. With regard to social welfare, for example, it has been argued that ' "vulnerability" is so loaded with political, moral and practical implications that it is potentially damaging to the pursuit of social justice' (Brown, 2011: 313).
7   The recommendations of which have not been implemented.

[8] See, for example, discussion of participation in the 'civil limb' European Court of Human Rights guidance on Article 6.

[9] The Criminal Procedure Rules 2015, www.legislation.gov.uk/uksi/2015/1490/contents/made

[10] Criminal Practice Directions 2015, www.judiciary.uk/wp-content/uploads/2015/09/crim-pd-2015.pdf

[11] The Family Procedure (Amendment No. 3) Rules 2017, www.legislation.gov.uk/uksi/2017/1033/made

[12] Practice Direction 3AA – Vulnerable persons: Participation in proceedings and giving evidence, www.justice.gov.uk/courts/procedure-rules/family/practice_directions/practice-direction-3aa-vulnerable-persons-participation-in-proceedings-and-giving-evidence

[13] The Tribunal Procedure (First-tier Tribunal) (Immigration and Asylum Chamber) Rules 2014, www.legislation.gov.uk/uksi/2014/2604/article/2/made

[14] The Employment Tribunals (Constitution and Rules of Procedure) Regulations 2013, www.legislation.gov.uk/uksi/2013/1237/schedule/1/made

[15] www.judiciary.uk/publications/new-edition-of-the-equal-treatment-bench-book-launched/

[16] UNCRPD – Articles, www.un.org/development/desa/disabilities/convention-on-the-rights-of-persons-with-disabilities/convention-on-the-rights-of-persons-with-disabilities-2.html

[17] Ethical approval for the research was obtained from Birkbeck's School of Law.

[18] Coroners have responsibility for hearing inquests into deaths which were violent, unnatural, unexplained or occurred in state detention. Close family of the deceased can attend the inquest as 'interested persons', which gives them the right to question witnesses (directly or through a legal representative) and to ask to see evidence in advance of the hearing. Recent years have seen a growing policy emphasis on ensuring that bereaved family members are 'at the heart of' the coronial process (see, for example, Ministry of Justice, 2013: 4 and 2019: 9).

References

Brown, K. (2011) ' "Vulnerability": handle with care', *Ethics and Social Welfare*, 5(3): 313–21.

European Court of Human Rights (2019) *Guide on Article 6 of the European Convention on Human Rights: Right to a Fair Trial (Criminal Limb)*, updated on 31 December 2019, Strasbourg: Council of Europe/European Court of Human Rights.

Fundamental Rights Agency (2016) *Handbook on European Law Relating to Access to Justice*, Vienna: European Union Agency for Fundamental Rights.

Judicial College (2018) *Equal Treatment Bench Book: February 2018 Edition (March 2020 Revision)*, London: Judicial College.

Law Commission (2016) *Unfitness to Plead: Summary*, London: Law Commission.

McKeever, G. (2020) 'Comparing courts and tribunals through the lens of legal participation', *Civil Justice Quarterly*, 39(3): 217–236.

Ministry of Justice (2013) *Implementing the Coroner Reforms in Part 1 of the Coroners and Justice Act 2009: Response to Consultation on Rules, Regulations, Coroner Areas and Statutory Guidance*, London: MoJ.

Ministry of Justice (2019) *Final Report: Review of Legal Aid for Inquests*, London: MoJ.

Owusu-Bempah, A. (2018) 'The interpretation and application of the right to effective participation', *International Journal of Evidence and Proof*, 22(4): 321–41.

von Wistinghausen, N. (2013) 'Victims as witnesses: views from the defence', in T. Bonacker and C. Safferling (eds) *Victims of International Crimes: An Interdisciplinary Discourse*, The Hague: TMC Asser Press, pp 165–173.

TWO

Policy and Practice Supporting Lay Participation

Gillian Hunter

This chapter sets the context for empirical findings discussed in Chapters Three and Four. It provides an overview of law, policy and practice intended to support and manage lay participation in courts and tribunals in England and Wales, and presents a brief account of change over the past two decades in the jurisdictions under study. This includes a description of the development and evaluation of special measures for vulnerable and intimidated court users, and the guidance available to practitioners to improve their communication with court users and support participation. In assessing the effects of these various forms of assistance and professional guidance, the limited research on lay users' experiences of court is examined. The chapter is framed by discussion of broader system issues, including reforms made to legal aid in 2012 and the courts modernisation programme in England and Wales, documenting how these factors are perceived to impact participation and access to justice. Additionally, reflecting the fact that the chapter was completed in May 2020 at the time of the UK's 'lockdown' in response to the COVID-19 pandemic, some questions are raised about supporting lay participation when physical attendance at court is largely ruled out.

Approach

Sources published between 2000 and 2020 were used to describe the policy and practice environment in England and Wales relating to lay participation. These comprised:

- research identified through searching electronic databases – Criminal Justice Abstracts and Westlaw UK – to locate studies on effectiveness of practice and court users' experiences;
- policy and practice guidance from government (for example, HM Courts and Tribunals Service (HMCTS), Ministry of Justice (MoJ), Crown Prosecution Service (CPS)), the judiciary and professional bodies (for example, the Law Society);
- wider commentary on lay participation and access to justice, including from advocacy and reform organisations.

Multiple jurisdictions are covered – the criminal and family courts, the Employment Tribunal (ET) and the First-tier Tribunal (Immigration and Asylum Chamber) (IAC). It is impossible within the space available to report on every matter pertinent to lay participation or to discuss in detail those issues which are included. Rather, the chapter gives an overview of key aspects of policy and procedure that may assist or challenge lay participation in judicial proceedings. In the following sections, the concept of court user vulnerability and its relevance to the development of practice across the courts is examined. The evolution of special measures is tracked – as a main example of processes being adapted for lay users – from their introduction in the criminal courts to their uptake elsewhere, and the evidence for the efficacy of these measures is reviewed. This is based mainly on developments in the criminal courts, where to date most research has focused. The development of professional practice and the extent to which this is changing to accommodate and support lay participation is examined. The key structural issues considered are access to state-funded legal representation as an important provision for 'equality of arms' when disputes reach the courts, and reforms introduced to digitise court processes and increase the use of virtual hearings in lieu of physical attendance at court.

Vulnerability

Factors shaping lay participation in the justice system extend beyond individual traits that might render a court user vulnerable so defined in narrow legal terms. Brown and colleagues (2017), for example, draw attention to the myriad ways in which vulnerability as a concept is discussed and understood, depending on disciplinary and theoretical perspective. Of note is how 'vulnerability' is deployed in different policy and practice contexts against normative standards that support narratives about 'deserving and un-deserving citizens' (Brown et al, 2017). This is especially pertinent when determining the allocation of state resources, where the focus is firmly on the individual rather than the structural processes and mechanisms that might make people 'vulnerable'.

The starting point for this review was how the 'vulnerable' court user is defined and here too it is possible to identify how the delineation of vulnerability sets out how far and for whom the courts are willing to adapt procedures to support lay participation.

Vulnerability of court participants is referred to in primary legislation concerning the criminal courts only, but has been the subject of procedure rules, practice directions and professional guidance across jurisdictions. Most recently, the Civil Justice Council (2020) consulted on the treatment of vulnerable witnesses and parties within civil proceedings, issuing a series of recommendations in order to better align assistance for vulnerable parties in civil courts with that provided in the criminal and family courts.

Vulnerability in law

Statutory 'tests' of vulnerability are set out in the Youth Justice and Criminal Evidence Act (YJCEA) 1999: with regard to witnesses (prosecution and defence) in the criminal courts and for defendants in the Police and Justice Act 2006 (s 47) and Coroners and Justice Act 2009 (s 104). These stipulate factors that may negatively affect meaningful participation in criminal proceedings – where it is deemed proper that a person should participate[1] – and thereby undermine the right to a fair trial[2] and access to justice (Jacobson, 2017).

The Act specifies that the court can take measures to support a vulnerable witness as defined under section 16 of the YJCEA (and similarly those defined as intimidated under section 17). Such witnesses are *eligible* for support, but an application to the court must be made, including how the measure will improve the quality of evidence. Factors that *may* elicit additional support from the criminal courts for a witness to give evidence are under section 16:

- age of under 18 years;
- mental disorder (defined by the Mental Health Act 1983);
- significant impairment of intelligence or social functioning;
- physical disability or disorder.

And under section 17:

- witnesses who are 'intimidated' (as opposed to 'vulnerable') and need assistance on grounds of fear or distress about testifying.

Some of these broad categories of vulnerability – aside from age – can be difficult to identify, to confirm or to make an objective assessment about their likely impact on participation (Jacobson, 2017; Owusu-Bempah, 2018). Ultimately, validating who is vulnerable becomes a matter of judgment for the courts, although other statutory agencies – for example, the police and CPS in the case of complainants and other witnesses in the criminal courts – have important roles in identifying and alerting the courts to lay users' needs.

Vulnerability among court users

Consistently, data on offenders' backgrounds suggest high levels of vulnerability as defined in the YJCEA, including mental health problems and learning difficulties (Jacobson et al, 2010). Studies have also highlighted higher rates of criminal victimisation among people with physical and learning disabilities and mental health problems compared to the general population, including experience of violent and sexual offences (Khalifeh et al, 2013; Pettit et al, 2013). Mr Justice Cobb,[3] in a speech to the Family Bar Association Conference in 2017, described the many forms of 'vulnerability' among parties in the Family Court, emphasising the mix of personal needs and wider circumstances that make people vulnerable in the context of judicial proceedings:

> Some exhibit their vulnerability visibly and unmistakably, others subtly, silently and discreetly. There are those whose vulnerability is defined by their age or mental incapacity. There are those who are paralysingly vulnerable because of the behaviours of others towards them, suffering intimidation and persecution. Some deliberately hide their vulnerability out of shame or fear; the spouse who bears the emotional and unhealed wounds of years of control and coercion. The cohort is populated with many others including those with learning difficulties, dyslexia, dyspraxia, behavioural disorders, with ADHD or Asperger's Syndrome, with autism, the list goes on.

Research conducted among immigration and asylum detainees underscores the importance of conceiving of vulnerability as fluid: something that can emerge over time, and which involves an interaction between an individual's experiences and pre-existing factors. It is stressed that vulnerability can relate as much to the nature of the legal system as to individuals' personal circumstances. For example, factors creating vulnerability among asylum seekers appearing before the IAC can include:

- having fled their country of origin because of war, persecution, harassment and discrimination;
- limited economic resources or social connections;
- inability to speak English;
- experiences of sexual abuse, ill-treatment and torture;
- feelings of anxiety, depression, trauma and/or suspicion of authority due to experiences.
  (See, for example, Blake, 2011; the Detention Forum's Vulnerable People Working Group, 2015; Royal College of Psychiatrists, 2016; Shaw, 2016.)

The ways in which vulnerability can be *created* or exacerbated by the justice process have also been noted in research on the criminal courts. For example, research on the Crown Court (Jacobson et al, 2015; Kirby, 2017) has highlighted the elaborate, ritualised and often archaic aspects to the contested trial which can make the process difficult, confusing and stressful. Further, it is argued that the adversarial system and rules for testing evidence in court can render all witnesses and defendants vulnerable to some extent, which can be experienced by some as a form of secondary victimisation (Wheatcroft et al, 2009).

Inequalities of power between lay participant and court, or lay claimant versus professional respondent, feature heavily in discussions of the ET (for example, Busby and McDermott, 2012). Such concerns are pertinent across the justice system, especially taking into account the increase in numbers self-representing after government cuts were made to publicly funded legal representation in 2012 (to be discussed later).

More generic barriers to participation underline court users' estrangement from the specialist knowledge, language and formality of court processes and the anxiety and stress experienced when having to enter such alien spaces to resolve disputes (McKeever, 2013). Even in tribunals, which are structured to be more accessible to the lay user than the court, differences in education, language, culture, communication skills and confidence, compounded by lack of availability or awareness of sources of information and advice about hearings, create wide disparities in how court users cope with adjudication processes (Genn et al, 2006).

Evolution of special measures

The aspiration to improve participation and access to justice informed much of the development of specialist support for those defined as vulnerable. Closely aligned with this, however, are more instrumental concerns, including how to ensure that witnesses and parties provide their 'best evidence' (Tribunals Judiciary, 2010). With regard to the criminal courts, there has also been political pressure to 'rebalance' the system in favour of victims, including by trying to give them a greater voice in proceedings and easing their experience of attending and giving evidence in court[4] (for example, MoJ, 2013, 2014; Crown Prosecution Service, 2016).

In the criminal courts

Adaptations to traditional court processes for vulnerable witnesses outlined in the YJCEA include provision for:

- giving evidence from behind a screen so witnesses cannot be seen by nor see the defendant – screens can also shield witnesses from the public gallery (s 23);

- giving evidence via live video-link to the courtroom from a room or building elsewhere, with a supporter if necessary (s 24);
- clearing the courtroom of public and press (s 25);
- lawyers and judges removing wigs and gowns (s 26);
- using a pre-recorded video statement as evidence-in-chief (s 27) or pre-recorded cross-examination and re-examination (s 28);
- receiving communication assistance via a witness intermediary[5] who facilitates communication for witnesses who experience communication difficulties (s 29) (see Wurtzel and Marchant (2017) for detail on the intermediary's role);
- using communication aids (s 30).

The legislative picture is complicated when trying to determine who is eligible for special measures. While the YJCEA explicitly excluded defendants from access to adaptations, subsequent legislation has extended some support to defendants. Provisions in the Police and Justice Act 2006 allow for a vulnerable defendant to give evidence by live-link, although with additional criteria to meet.[6] The Coroners and Justice Act 2009 *would* permit access to an intermediary to aid communication during testimony, but this is not yet in force (see Chapter Five). Aside from those defined through statute, there are wider obligations on the courts to make adjustments for witnesses and defendants, as stipulated in case law, Criminal Practice Directions and Criminal Procedure Rules (to be discussed later).

Evaluating special measures in the criminal courts

Research examining special measures in the criminal courts has tended to focus on whether legislative objectives are being met, including through: identification of the need for measures and whether they are requested in time; levels of judicial agreement to measures; and their effects as perceived by court users. Resource constraints and the differential support for defendants and witnesses have also been examined.

For witnesses, the police and CPS must identify early in case preparation the need for special measures and apply to the courts. Several studies, involving case file reviews and practitioner interviews, have highlighted problems with this process, resulting in late applications or missed opportunities to apply. Commonly, this involved failure to identify need, poor information exchange between the police and CPS, and lack of detail about vulnerabilities in supporting paperwork (Burton et al, 2006; McCleod et al, 2010; Charles, 2012).

Cooper (2017), commenting on an appeal court case (*R. v G* [2017] EWCA Crim 617), highlighted continuing problems with how 'vulnerability' criteria are understood and applied in court, despite the concept of the 'vulnerable witness' being over 20 years old.[7] The case in question illustrates the blurred line between determinations of 'vulnerability' and 'intimidation'. Analysis of CPS data on outcomes of special measures applications in the early days (2003–2004) suggested that when vulnerability was identified and a timely application made to the courts, most were successful (Roberts et al, 2005). Reasons for refusal were most commonly noted as at 'judge's discretion' (based on matters of law), for example, where it was felt that the statutory criteria had not been met or because the application was late. A small number were rejected on pragmatic grounds, including lack of facilities at court (Roberts et al, 2005).

Research on witnesses' experiences of measures has generally found positive responses. Survey feedback from 569 vulnerable and intimidated witnesses attending criminal courts during 2003 (video recorded testimony and intermediaries were not available then) showed that those who received special measures were less likely to report feeling anxious or distressed. A third also said that they would have been unwilling to give evidence without them (Hamlyn et al, 2004). Burton and colleagues (2006) found that video-recorded evidence and the live video-link were highly regarded by witnesses and practitioners, although some practitioners had reservations about televised evidence because they thought it was less convincing than evidence given in person.

Witness intermediaries were piloted in six areas between 2004 and 2005 (Plotnikoff and Woolfson, 2007) before national roll-out in 2007. The evaluation showed that intermediaries were viewed positively by those who had used them, including for their help in identifying witnesses' communication difficulties. However, poor awareness and misunderstanding of eligibility criteria for appointing intermediaries, over-estimation of advocates' competence to question effectively, and under-estimation of witnesses' communication needs were identified as factors likely to inhibit wider uptake.

Ground rules hearings – introduced into the Criminal Practice Directions in 2013 and then the Criminal Procedure Rules in 2014 – were devised as part of intermediary training. They are a means by which the intermediary (ratified by the judge) pre-trial can inform the style and format of an advocate's questions to a witness to help understanding. These hearings are now used routinely for court users who have been identified as vulnerable or as having communication needs. Adaptations to the trial process can also be agreed in ground rules hearings; for example, how the intermediary will alert the court if the witness requires a break (Cooper et al, 2015). However, research on the conduct of hearings is limited, and there is evidence that practice varies on who is present, the extent of judicial direction on how the case will be put to the witness, and whether or not written questions are requested by the judge in advance (Cooper et al, 2015). On this last point, the practice of submitting cross-examination questions in advance for judicial vetting has become more widespread where a witness is young or vulnerable, and is not limited to hearings using intermediaries or those conducted under s28 (to be discussed later) as noted in *R* v *Zafer Dinc* [2017] EWCA Crim 1206.

Demand for intermediaries in England and Wales has grown. The latest annual report on the Witness Intermediary Scheme (MoJ, 2019a) reports that 6276 requests were made for a registered intermediary in the financial year 2018/19 (a monthly average of 523), representing a 190 per cent increase in requests since 2013/14. The majority were for child witnesses (47 per cent) followed by witnesses with learning disabilities (34 per cent), mental illness (13 per cent) and physical disabilities (6 per cent). Ninety-six per cent of requests were matched with an intermediary.

The last special measure to be introduced (s28 of the YJCEA) allows for a vulnerable witness's cross-examination and re-examination to be recorded in advance of the trial. This was piloted in three Crown Courts from 2014 and had been expanded to a further five sites by June 2019.[8]

During piloting, 194 s28 cases, mainly involving sexual offences, were dealt with. (Baverstock, 2016; Plotnikoff and Woolfson, 2016). Evaluation findings indicated continuing problems about awareness of eligibility criteria for special measures among the police and CPS, resulting in missed opportunities for pre-recording of evidence and cross-examination. There were reports of technological problems including poor visibility and sound quality of witnesses on screen. Findings suggested some positive outcomes, including practitioners' views that the experience of cross-examination was less stressful, and that questioning was more focused where ground rules hearings had been used to prepare questions. Trial lengths were shorter on average when using s28, and cross-examination took place earlier, which had benefits for witness recall (Baverstock, 2016).

In contrast to provisions for witnesses, there has been criticism of poor progress and late implementation of legislation affording special measures for defendants. This underlines the inequity of provision for vulnerable defendants compared to vulnerable witnesses, not least because the imbalance flouts compliance with rights legislation[9] and the courts' safeguarding responsibilities (e.g. Burton et al, 2006; Bradley, 2009; Tonry, 2010; Fairclough, 2016, 2018).

Jacobson and Talbot (2009), in research that reviewed court provision for adult defendants with learning disabilities, highlighted inadequate processes for identifying learning needs, including lack of specificity in defining learning difficulty and its conflation with mental illness. They also noted that defendants' exercise of their right to a fair trial and their meaningful participation was hindered by limited provision of support services before and during court hearings.

Despite the 2009 statute, vulnerable defendants still do not have access to the MoJ-registered intermediary scheme, nor rights to funding for this, with courts required to use their inherent powers to direct assistance from an intermediary for a defendant. There is no requirement for these intermediaries to be registered, meaning that they are not accredited, funded or regulated by the MoJ (Cooper and Wurtzel, 2013). More recent revisions to Criminal Practice Directions (in 2016) have further downgraded access to an intermediary for defendants, noting the measure to be 'rare' for testimony, but 'very rare' for the whole trial (Hoyano and Rafferty, 2017). It is further stated in directions that there is no presumption that a defendant should receive assistance, and even where an intermediary would improve the trial process, access is not a given. This underscores the prioritising of witnesses' access to intermediaries – as a costly resource. The guidance is laid out in *R* v *Rashid* [2017] EWCA Crim 2, whereby the rarity of a defendant having an intermediary's support throughout trial is reiterated, with the onus placed on the advocate to be able to ask a defendant questions in an appropriate and comprehensible manner.

Research conducted with a small sample of criminal lawyers identified three barriers to defendants gaining access to livelinks to give evidence (the other statutory provision for vulnerable defendants). These were: lack of awareness among defence lawyers that this was available for defendants; poor identification of vulnerability and a view that it was not tactically advantageous to have defendants give evidence in this way (Fairclough, 2016).

In the Family Court

There is no statutory definition of vulnerability in the Family Court, but there has been strong support for reforming practice in this area. The Family Justice Review[10] (2011) recommended that government and judiciary 'actively consider how children and vulnerable witnesses may be protected when giving evidence in family proceedings' (Family Justice Review Panel, 2011: 24). The judicial response to the review (Ryder, 2012)[11] suggested changes to practice directions to offer guidance on how an incapacitated adult party might be represented and how to identify and ask for special measures for vulnerable parties. In addition, these documents stressed the importance of the 'child's voice' in proceedings, whereas it was previously considered detrimental for a child to give oral evidence. This referenced the need to comply with the United Nations Convention on the Rights of the Child (1989) through judges ensuring the child's understanding of proceedings, that their wishes have been ascertained and that the court's final decision is explained to them.

The 'child's voice' is mainly represented through the Children and Family Court Advisory and Support Service (Cafcass), introduced in 2001 by the Criminal Justice and Court Services Act 2000. Cafcass advisors are trained social workers whose role is to safeguard and promote the welfare of children; give advice to the court about applications; make provision for children to be represented; and provide information and support to children and their families. Ofsted's[12] latest inspection of Cafcass (2018) rated the service as 'outstanding', noting that listening to and understanding children and acting on their views was well embedded in practice in both public and private law.

The position on children's non-participation in family proceedings was successfully challenged (*Re W (Children) (Abuse: Oral Evidence)* [2010] UKSC 12). In response, the Supreme Court concluded that there should no longer be a presumption against children giving oral evidence, but left it open for the Court to determine its position on a case-by-case basis, and to decide what practical steps should be taken to accommodate children giving evidence.

Sir James Munby (President of the Family Division from 2013 to 2018) has vigorously highlighted the Family Court's shortcomings in accommodating children's voices and views when considering their 'best interests', and has extended this criticism to provision for all parties who are vulnerable in some way (see, for example, Munby, 2016). He declared the Family Court to be 'shamefully behind' the criminal courts in this regard and set up the Vulnerable Witnesses and Children's Working Group (VWCWG) to review guidelines on involving children in proceedings, address the wider needs of vulnerable people in the Family Court and establish how best to adapt provisions and developments from the criminal courts to the Family Division, including through revising Family Procedure Rules and practice directions.

The resulting report from the VWCWG (Judiciary of England and Wales, 2015) noted the high prevalence of vulnerability among parties in the Family Court. It also highlighted ongoing concerns about the lack of resources for provision of intermediaries and government reforms that made most private law cases ineligible for legal aid, thus increasing numbers of litigants in person (LiPs) in the Family Court. These funding changes had also made it more likely for abuse complainants to be cross-examined in court by their alleged abusers;[13] something which was reported to be happening all too frequently and which received attention[14] from lawyers' professional associations, the charity Women's Aid and commentators in the media who were incredulous that such practice was being allowed to persist.

For example, data collected over three months during 2015, from 89 per cent of Family Court centres in England and Wales, identified 124 hearings where there was actual or potential cross-examination of a vulnerable or intimidated witness by a LiP accused of domestic abuse (Corbett and Summerfield, 2017). Qualitative interviews with 15 family judges explored management of such cases and identified the use of screens, remote video-links or judicial intervention to relay questions from the LiP to the witness. This last technique, however, raised concerns among judges about maintaining impartiality in proceedings and they called for clearer guidance on appropriate case management practices. Latterly, legislation included in the Domestic Offences Bill (Home Office, 2019–21)[15] prohibits perpetrators of domestic and other forms of abuse from cross-examining their victims in person in the Family Court and will also prevent victims from having to cross-examine their abusers. This additionally gives the court discretion to prevent cross-examination in person where it would diminish the quality of the witness's evidence or cause the witness significant distress.

Family Procedure Rule 3A and accompanying Practice Direction 3AA took effect in November 2017, underlining the court's duty to be aware, and take account, of a range of factors that might impact on a court user's ability to participate effectively in proceedings. These include:

- actual or perceived intimidation by another party, witness or their wider family or associates;
- a mental disorder or significant impairment of intelligence or social functioning;
- a physical disability or disorder;
- the age, level of maturity, and ethnic, social, cultural and religious background and domestic circumstances;
- any issues arising in proceedings, including concerns in relation to abuse.

Nevertheless, the courts' ability to support participation appears to be tempered. Commentators have highlighted the absence in the amended rules of powers to ensure public funding for certain measures. For example, MoJ guidance to family courts stressed that there was no statutory requirement for HMCTS to fund an intermediary or intermediary assessment in family proceedings.[16] Thus, while there is the option for specialist support, its use continues to be constrained (Cooper, 2018).

In the Employment Tribunal

In general, tribunals are intended to be much less formal than the courts and to operate in ways that should facilitate lay participation. For example, Sir Andrew Leggatt's review of tribunals (2001) suggested that lay users should be able to present their case without the need for expert legal representation, through support from external advice services and with the assistance of tribunal staff and judiciary who have expertise in tribunal jurisdictions.

It has been argued that the ET can exercise a relatively high level of discretion to accommodate vulnerability. Cooper and Arnold (2017: 5), for example, explain that the ET 'can and does adjust procedures to remove barriers to effective participation of witnesses and parties at oral hearings'. Case management discussions are used to determine what adjustments are needed for vulnerable and intimated parties and reasonable adjustments can then be made to questioning, language, giving evidence and provision of support and intermediaries.

The Employment Tribunal (Constitution and Rules Procedure) Regulations 2004 confer wide procedural discretion through provisions, including:

- so far as practicable, ensuring that parties are on an equal footing and that the case is dealt with fairly: regulation 3(1) and (2)(a) and (c);

- powers to manage proceedings that mean the judge may at any time, either on application of a party, or on their own initiative, make an order in relation to any matter which appears to be appropriate (for example, these may concern the manner in which the proceedings are to be conducted);
- the judge can seek to avoid formality in proceedings, not be bound by any enactment or rule of law relating to the admissibility of evidence in proceedings: rule 14(2);
- the judge or tribunal shall make such inquiries of persons appearing and of the witnesses as considered appropriate and shall otherwise conduct the hearing in the manner she considers most appropriate for the clarification of issues and generally for the just handling of the proceedings: rule 14(3).

The case law examples cited in the following paragraphs illustrate how procedural discretion is used to ensure parties have a fair hearing and can participate. These stress that it is up to the ET to investigate and make decisions based upon evidence and circumstances of the case and parties, and to draw upon expert opinion as required regarding the need for adaptations. However, it is also contingent on the parties' acceptance of adjustments, and the implications for fairness to both sides need to be factored into assessments and any adjustments made.

In accounting for intimidation and distress, *Duffy* v *George* [2013] EWCA Civ 908 demonstrates the court's powers to allow parties to give evidence in the absence of one another. Case law relating to procedural adjustments for disability or ill health among parties include *JW Rackham* v *NHS Professionals Ltd* [2015] UKEAT/0110/15/LA, which concerned a claimant with Asperger's Syndrome (Cooper and Arnold, 2017). Here, the ET obtained a GP's report and sought expert advice to determine the procedural adjustments required. Adjustments to the hearing, including to cross-examination, were agreed by the parties and endorsed by the claimant's GP.

The following examples, however, suggest a lack of consistency in how thorough the ET is expected to be in assessing the need for adjustments to ensure fairness. In *Hak* v *St Christopher's Fellowship* [2015] UKEAT 0446/14/DA, the claimant was a non-native English speaker making a claim about unfair treatment and racial discrimination at work. He requested an interpreter, but none was found and when asked whether he was happy to proceed, he said 'yes'. After losing the case, he appealed, but this was dismissed on grounds that he said he had been happy to proceed, so there was no unfairness or procedural irregularity. In *Galo* v *Bombardier Aerospace UK* [2016] NICA 25, the Northern Ireland Court of Appeal held that the tribunal had not provided a fair trial to a claimant with Asperger's Syndrome because it failed to make reasonable adjustments for his disability and medical circumstances when he was a LiP. The court adjudged a more active approach was required, stating that inquiries should have been made about any necessary procedural adjustments in light of his disability. It criticised the tribunal for failing to obtain a medical report or arrange for a doctor to attend the hearing. It was also stated that the tribunal should have taken note of the *Equal Treatment Bench Book* (ETBB) that provides guidance for all judges on addressing the difficulties experienced by vulnerable litigants.

The ETBB 2018 published by the Judicial College advises that ground rules hearings should be conducted to consider adjustments for participation and that expert evidence might be needed to assist decision making. Matters which can be considered at such a hearing when a person is 'vulnerable' include:

- approach to questioning and cross-examination – how it is controlled, and tone, language and duration of questioning;
- a full explanation of court procedures for an applicant with a disability or LIP and advice on availability of pro-bono assistance and voluntary sector help;
- the need for extra time for those with learning disabilities to ensure they have understood;
- language and vocabulary;

- whether the respondent's counsel should offer cross-examination and questions in writing to assist the claimant.

In the Immigration and Asylum Chamber

Guidance for IAC judiciary encourages the use of discretion to respond to the needs of vulnerable appellants to ensure they receive a fair hearing. For example, a Practice Direction issued in 2008 for first and upper tribunal (child and sensitive witnesses)[17] allowed children and vulnerable adults, as defined in the Safeguarding and Vulnerable Groups Act 2006, and 'sensitive' witnesses, whose quality of evidence might be diminished due to fear or distress, to give evidence via telephone, video-link or other means and to be supported if required by a skilled individual. The direction also urges judges to consider the need for calling a witness where this might be prejudicial to their welfare.

Further guidance (Joint Presidential Guidance for Tribunals Judiciary, Note 2) was issued in 2010 encouraging judges to be proactive, emphasising they should use their discretion to determine what adjustments might be needed for vulnerable appellants. The guidance is premised upon the notion that effective communication and comprehension is essential to the legal process, and that vulnerable appellants may require measures, adaptations or procedures to enable participation. It is acknowledged that without identifying or accounting for vulnerability, the quality of evidence may be compromised. Judges are guided to account for vulnerability before, during and after the hearing, when making decisions and weighing up the evidence. A range of factors are listed as potentially creating vulnerability, which may vary in terms of nature, extent and impact, and may be hidden or emerge over time. These factors are for the judge to assess and may relate to:

- mental health;
- social or learning difficulties;

- religious beliefs or practices;
- sexual orientation;
- ethnic, social and cultural background;
- domestic or employment circumstances;
- physical disability or impairment.

Vulnerability may relate to extraneous factors, including experiences of detention or torture. Judges are directed to identify vulnerabilities at a case management meeting, or at the beginning of the substantive hearing, to seek expert evidence where necessary, to take into account the needs and wishes of the vulnerable person, to consider what adjustments are required, and to anticipate behavioural difficulties or challenges that may arise in the hearing.

Measures and discretionary actions by the judge may include seeking agreement on key areas of dispute pre-hearing; allowing a representative or supporting adult to identify concerns about well-being; restricting public or family members' access to the hearing to ensure evidence can be given freely; speaking clearly and jargon-free; curtailing aggressive cross-examination; ensuring questioning is tailored to age and maturity; ensuring the appellant has understood and is allowed breaks; and adjourning the case if vulnerability emerges in the course of the hearing, in order to seek expert advice about its impact.

The guidance states that vulnerable appellants may require more time to understand and think about questions and may be easily influenced. Inconsistencies and contradictions may indicate a lack of understanding and/or power imbalances. Factors underlying vulnerability may affect comprehension, articulation and so forth, and so should be taken into account when assessing evidence and making decisions.

A Court of Appeal case – *UK – AM (Afghanistan)* v *Secretary of State for the Home Department* [2017] EWCA Civ 1123 – concerning an asylum claim by a 17-year-old male, illustrates how practice directions and guidance about accommodating vulnerable appellants in the IAC are upheld. The appeal was granted on the grounds that the tribunal had failed to follow expert advice about the ground rules that were needed during the hearing to account for the appellant's learning difficulty, but also that the Joint Presidential Guidance Notes (2010) stressing the importance of the best interests of the child had been ignored.

Guidance for practitioners and judges

Guidance for practitioners addresses 'professional culture' in courts and tribunals in relation to the participation of court users.

The Advocate's Gateway[18] (TAG, founded in 2013) hosts resources, including 'toolkits' that offer guidance on communicating with young and vulnerable court users. There are toolkits written for the criminal, family and civil courts and those that focus on questioning people with specific communication needs, such as autism. The toolkits detail evidenced advice on question format, language to use or avoid and the importance of body language, and they provide links to source materials and examples of good and bad practice for eliciting testimony. Data from Google Analytics on 'traffic' to the TAG website between March 2019 and February 2020 show in total 18,755 'visits' were made to the ten most viewed toolkits on TAG.

There is some evidence from the criminal courts that such guidance is having a positive effect. Research commissioned by the Bar Standards Board and the Solicitors Regulation Authority (Hunter et al, 2018) comprised interviews with 46 circuit judges and four High Court judges across England and Wales about their perceptions of the quality of criminal advocacy. While many respondents were critical of advocacy, an area of practice that was said to be improving was skills in questioning vulnerable witnesses, and TAG was sometimes name-checked in these discussions.

Guidance for judges found in the ETBB (Judicial College, 2018) emphasises judicial responsibility for ensuring fair and equal treatment for court users. It includes sections on special measures and seeks to raise awareness of the potential effects of a wide range of physical and mental disabilities and ethnic, cultural, religious and socio-economic factors on court users' capacity to understand and engage in court processes. It offers guidance on identifying and accommodating these various needs to support more effective participation. However, the extent to which the guidance is applied is unknown.

As is clear from previous sections, much of how the courts accommodate lay participation is determined by practice directions and procedure rules, by appellate decisions and through professional convention. In the criminal courts, for example, practice regarding vulnerability among witnesses and defendants has evolved through Criminal Practice Directions which emphasise requirements to take 'every reasonable step' to facilitate participation of witnesses and defendants to give their best evidence, and also to enable defendants' understanding of proceedings so they can engage fully with their defence. The Practice Directions also underline judicial responsibility for controlling cross-examination of a vulnerable witness or defendant (including preventing over-rigorous or repetitive questioning) and the option of departing from traditional forms of cross-examination if required.

Henderson (2016: 181), discussing criminal trial management, describes the attitudes of judges and advocates – rather than legislation or government policy – as 'the single most important factor in achieving any sort of change'. Her interviews with judges, advocates and intermediaries show that while judges recognise the need to manage trials dealing with vulnerable witnesses and defendants, some remain reticent about doing so, perceiving intervention to threaten their neutral role. This echoed concerns raised by a Judicial Working Group (2013) convened to assess how best to accommodate LiPs. The group sought further training for judges to better prepare them for managing LiPs, and amendments to Practice Directions to allow for a more inquisitorial approach in cases where at least one party is unrepresented. Indeed, an updated section in the ETBB offers practical guidance on supporting LiPs while 'holding the confidence of both sides' (2018: 30).

The tribunal process is intended to be more inquisitorial than adversarial (McKeever, 2020). Thomas (2013) describes an 'active enabling approach' to hearing evidence from lay participants, which can be achieved by creating the right atmosphere – not overly formal – and assisting the appellant to bring out the relevant issues in the case; something that is especially important when dealing with unrepresented parties. Indeed, claims as to the inquisitorial nature of tribunals and their ability to manage unrepresented parties have been deployed by government in defence of cuts to funding for legal advice and representation – arguments that Thomas (2013) asserts are over-blown. He notes that while there is a move away from traditional adversarial approaches, this varies and depends on the individual judge's approach and experience in drawing out evidence; further, procedures in some tribunals (he cites both the IAC and ET here) remain largely adversarial.

While lay participants may not experience tribunals as informal in tone (Genn et al, 2006; McKeever, 2013), interviews with tribunal users identify factors which encourage lay participation, including help to understand the process and what is required, recognition that low levels of prior knowledge are likely, and support with setting out their case. While judicial input is key, so too is the role of tribunal staff and others who offer advice and moderate user expectations before a hearing (McKeever, 2013).

This highlights the importance of judicial practice in supporting lay users, but also of the role played by other practitioners; it is professional understandings of and attitudes to lay participation that are the subject of the empirical research discussed in the next chapter of this volume. Judicial discretion is frequently invoked in rules and directions about accommodating vulnerable court users and LiPs in courts and tribunals. In proposed court reforms (to be discussed later), judicial discretion is cited as central to decision making about what types of hearing can be heard by telephone, via video or in person.[19]

One recent observational study of judicial discretion in IAC hearings (Gill et al, 2017) suggests a range of dynamics are at play and that judges use their discretion in ways that variously ameliorate or exacerbate the impact of vulnerability, or otherwise convey their indifference. Analysis of 290 IAC cases showed that helpful behaviours were less common than indifferent or exacerbating behaviours and that factors including gender of judge (female), appellant age (under 18 and over 50), day of the week (helpful discretionary actions declined over the course of the week) and appellant gender (male) were associated with more helpful behaviours. The authors note that there may be some ways judges seek to help that are less observable, and court users, judges and legal professionals may differ in their perceptions of what kinds of behaviours are more or less helpful.

Equality of arms

The Legal Aid, Sentencing and Punishment of Offenders Act 2012 (LASPO) came into force in 2013. The legislation was intended to reduce the stated £2 billion annual costs of publicly funded legal representation as part of government plans to reduce the fiscal deficit (MoJ, 2010). LASPO removed funding for legal advice and representation for areas of law, including most employment law, non-asylum immigration cases and most private family law cases. For criminal cases, means testing[20] to determine eligibility for legal aid has been in place in the magistrates' court since 2006 and in the Crown Court since 2010 and is set out in LASPO,[21] although thresholds for legal aid are currently under review (MoJ, 2019b). In brief, it is available to all defendants under 18 years of age and adults with a disposable household income of under £12,475. An income of up to £22,325 allows for funding – if the additional interest of justice test is met – for cases in both magistrates' and Crown courts, and between £22,325 and £37,500 for legal aid in the Crown Court, although this might cover only partial costs. Further, funding will only be granted for cases in a magistrates' court where it is deemed 'in the interest of justice' for the defendant to be represented. Guidance from the Legal Aid Agency (2018) to improve consistency of decision making in staff assessments about the interests of justice outlines the following key factors:

- if there is high risk to liberty, livelihood or serious damage to reputation if proceedings go against the defendant;
- whether proceedings involve consideration of a substantial question of law;
- difficulty for the defendant in understanding and presenting their case;
- if the case involves expert cross-examination of a prosecution witness.

The guidance stresses the principle of 'equality of arms' whereby a defendant must have an effective opportunity to present their case to the court and not be placed at a substantial disadvantage in relation to the prosecution. This emphasises a case's legal complexity rather than concerns about equality of arms between lay court user and legal practitioner.

A narrative review of international research on LiPs in the family and civil courts (since 1990), undertaken to assess the *likely* impacts of LASPO reforms (Williams, 2011), found that LiPs tended to be younger and have lower levels of income and education than those who were represented. An earlier study on these same courts found that a significant minority were vulnerable, defined as being a victim of violence or having substance misuse or mental health problems (Moorhead and Sefton, 2005). LiPs were reported to have difficulties understanding evidential requirements or identifying legally relevant facts and could find the court process overwhelming. The support they required to navigate hearings created extra work for practitioners, but also raised questions about what help could be offered while maintaining impartiality. Williams (2011) stressed the lack of research on case outcomes for LiPs compared to those with legal representation, but contended that the weight of available evidence suggested these were poorer for LiPs.

Litigants bringing certain types of cases to court – including the IAC and Family Court – are required to pay court fees in addition to, where necessary, funding their own legal representation.[22] Two Justice Committee inquiries (2015; 2016) have found that court charges subvert access to justice for lay users, raising crucial questions about how government efforts to reduce public expenditure are balanced against efforts to preserve legal rights and access to justice.

Criminal Court fees for defendants of between £150 and £1,200 were introduced in April 2015, including a higher fee for those convicted after a not guilty plea. These were found to have perverse effects, including incentivising guilty pleas among those wishing to avoid the risk of paying the higher charge if later found guilty. Further, doubts were raised about whether monies owed could be successfully collected, given the limited financial means of many defendants. The fees were scrapped by December 2015. Between 2013 and 2017, claimants were charged for making a claim to the ET (Pyper et al, 2017). The inquiry into court and tribunal fees (2016) found that their introduction was associated with a substantial fall in cases being brought and there were concerns about the impact of fees on those of low means and pregnant women, and the resultant 'inequality of arms' between individuals and small businesses on the one hand and the state and major companies on the other. There was also concern that discrimination claims in particular were being deterred by the potentially substantial proportion of any award that the fees represented. In July 2017, the Supreme Court ruled that ET fees were unlawful under UK and EU law as they prevented access to justice (*R (on the application of Unison) (Appellant)* v *Lord Chancellor* [2017] UKSC 51). This was supported by evidence that would-be claimants often cited fees as their reason for not pursuing a claim.

Impacts of legal aid reforms

Assessments of the effects of reforms to legal aid have indicated that any savings accrued to the public purse were outweighed by costs to the courts of managing increasing numbers of cases where one or both parties were unrepresented (National Audit Office, 2014; Law Society, 2017). A review by the Law Society of the impact of civil legal aid reforms cited evidence of their 'corrosive impact on access to justice' (2017: 2), collating a range of data to highlight the consequences: the increased numbers of vulnerable people in non–criminal cases who no longer had access to legal aid, continuing barriers for those who were eligible because of significant gaps in availability of legal advice and services, and the wider negative impacts on society of unresolved disputes.

In 2019, the President of the Family Division, Sir Andrew McFarlane, launched a review of the Family Court, noting the burden on the court of the growing number of LiPs in private law disputes. He also emphasised the difficulties faced by the judiciary who had to manage often 'emotionally charged' LiPs.[23] Routine data collated from the Family Court for the period July to September 2019 (MoJ, 2019c) showed that the proportion of disposals where neither applicant nor respondent had legal representation was 39 per cent: an increase of 25 per cent since 2013.

The increasing presence of LiPs in the courts throws into sharp relief the problem of overly complex courtroom language and the need for court procedures to be made clearer to lay people in order that they can participate effectively (JUSTICE, 2019). Research carried out by the Law for Life

Advice Project (2014) identified information needs of LiPs that were not being properly addressed, including with regard to the role of the court, court processes, legal language and the law. They recommended that all new court materials or those that require updating should be made suitable for LiPs and suggested that bespoke 'how to' guides should be produced, including on case preparation. Building professional capacity in designing and writing materials for lay participants was noted as fundamental to supporting LiPs.

Court users' experiences of self-representing

On the basis of research involving interviews and observations in family and civil courts in Northern Ireland – where procedures are similar to those in England and Wales – McKeever and colleagues (2018) identify three main barriers to participation: a dearth of pre-hearing information and advice for LiPs about how to self-represent; linked to this, a lack of awareness among LiPs of their knowledge deficits; and understandable difficulties in separating emotion from legal argument.

Trinder and colleagues (2014) conducted 151 case studies across five family courts during four weeks in 2013. Each comprised observation, interviews with parties and professionals involved and review of case files. Cases were sampled to include different hearing types and those involving represented and unrepresented parties. While highlighting commonalities with LiPs before LASPO, a crucial difference was the increasing numbers who were unrepresented because of inability to pay rather than by choice. Of the LiPs in their study, most had difficulties with court procedures and the legal issues involved in their cases; noted even for those with higher levels of education or professional experience. Approximately half were vulnerable in some way, making self-representation even more difficult. Issues faced by the courts included refusal by some LiPs to engage with proceedings, and – infrequent – aggressive or disruptive behaviour.

Lee and Tkacukova (2017) surveyed nearly 200 LiPs at Birmingham Civil Justice Centre during four weeks in 2016, half of whom were attending the Family Court. Just under two thirds said they had no qualifications or had left school prior to A-levels and over half received state benefits. The authors use these data to highlight potential vulnerability and limited capacity to fund legal advice or representation or to self-represent effectively. For the subset of respondents trying to resolve private family law matters, most reported having undertaken no advance preparation for their hearing.

The numbers of defendants self-representing in magistrates' courts is unknown, but the view among magistrates and lawyers interviewed[24] for a small study (Transform Justice, 2016) is that their number is increasing. Interviewees noted three reasons for this: ineligibility for legal aid or difficulties proving eligibility; lack of awareness of legal rights or of the importance of seeking legal advice; and poor organisation associated with defendants' often chaotic lives. Self-representation was described as impeding defendants' effective participation throughout the court process and the achievement of just outcomes. The main problems were said to be:

- limited ability to understand charges, and to assess the strength of the case against them in deciding how to plea;
- lack of understanding of the difference between defence and mitigation;
- anxiety about self-representing;
- unreliable systems for sending or receiving paperwork, exclusion from digital systems;
- lack of understanding of the rules of evidence;
- lack of experience in conducting cross-examination.

Concern was expressed by interviewees about the limited opportunity for identifying vulnerability among self-representing defendants, as needs and requirements for adaptations to support participation tend to be raised with the court on a defendant's behalf by their lawyer.

LiPs in the Crown Court are rarer, although recent figures show an increase since 2010 in those self-representing at first hearing.[25] Such cases are also said to be more time consuming for judiciary and court staff who have to adjust practice to accommodate defendants' lack of understanding (Thompson and Becker, 2019).

Kirk and colleagues (2015) have challenged government claims of ET litigants being too quick to raise applications, or bringing weak or vexatious claims, as a rationale for funding cuts and ET charges. Their study of over 150 workers seeking redress for work-related grievances between 2012 and 2014 found that significant barriers existed prior to the introduction of fees.

Busby and McDermott (2012) interviewed ten non-unionised employees who could not afford legal advice and had used the Citizens Advice Bureau (CAB) for support with their dispute. The study showed how the formality of the ET process was intimidating to claimants. The authors suggested that while the CAB could help rectify some power imbalances by explaining processes and supporting claimants with completing forms, a lack of claimant representation can produce inequality as employers tend to be represented. Similar findings were noted in a survey of 500 low-paid, non-unionised employees (Pollert, 2010). This study uncovered stories of powerlessness among claimants and resistance and obfuscation among employers, which meant that cases were often dropped as they became too stressful or difficult to pursue. Pollert (2010: 74) argued that, at all stages, claimants' experiences suggested that detailed, specialist evidence and cross-examination would have been needed to mount a serious challenge; elements that were beyond the means and capacity of many of the claimants. Both the Pollert (2010) and Busby and McDermott (2012) studies highlight imbalances of power as jeopardising access to justice for ET claimants, especially employees who lack financial means and legal or union representation.

Describing a 'crisis', the Bach Commission[26] (2017) outlined three main issues affecting 'everyday' access to justice post LASPO: the reduction in scope of legal aid and 'stringent' eligibility criteria to receive funding; a shrinking advice and information sector; and reduced numbers of legal practitioners willing to carry out legally aided work because of its limited availability, low fees and the increased bureaucracy that must be negotiated in order to obtain funding. The Commission argued that problems with access to justice have become so widespread – the report cites numerous examples collected as evidence – that there is a need for a 'Right to Justice Act' to codify the right to receive funded legal assistance, including early advice and legal representation across jurisdictions, and a Justice Commission to monitor and enforce such rights.

The government's current review of legal support (MoJ, 2019c) proffers actions to address concerns, linked into wider court reforms. These include simplifying application processes and raising awareness about access to and eligibility for aid, promoting methods of earlier resolution and enhancing support for LiPs, including by increasing funding for more face-to-face legal support.

Court reform programme and access to justice

The government court reform programme was launched in 2016 by the Ministry of Justice and Senior Judiciary with the stated aim of improving the accessibility and efficiency of the justice system (MoJ, 2016). It was announced as a £1 billion programme of work comprising 50 different projects to bring new technologies and modern ways of working to the courts and tribunals.[27] The National Audit Office (2018) has since questioned the government's ability to deliver reforms, citing scale and costs of the technological and cultural change that is being proposed. Other commentators focus more specifically on the effects of various reforms on lay users of the justice system.[28]

Court users are certainly central to the rhetoric of reform with targets to 'simplify' procedures and to design systems for users rather than professionals (MoJ, 2016; HMCTS, 2019). Key components involve replacing many paper processes with online forms and procedures and increasing the use of remote attendance (via use of video and telephone) to replace physical attendance at court. Criticism of proposals question government intentions, highlighting cost and efficiency savings rather than needs of court users as the greater stimuli. The following discussion reviews the reaction to reforms and their potential effects on lay experiences of justice, highlighting also the extraordinary circumstances of conducting court business at the time of COVID-19.

Remote court attendance

Use of video-enabled participation (live and pre-recorded) is established and largely well-regarded as a special measure to protect and reduce anxiety and stress among vulnerable and intimidated court users in the criminal and family courts. Beyond this, use of video technology in the criminal courts has been significantly expanded as part of the reform process. For example, defendants frequently appear from police stations or prison for first, or interim or sentencing hearings (but not, to date, for trials). Here, it has the benefit of reducing costs of prison processing and transportation of prisoners, often for long distances to attend short hearings. In the Family Court, piloting is underway of live video hearings dealing with applications for injunctions by victims of domestic abuse who can appear from their solicitors' offices (HMCTS, 2019). However, there is limited research on the effects of virtual hearings on the justice process, including how lay participants engage with the court and vice versa, and crucially how appearing virtually as opposed to being physically present may affect outcomes. Research conducted by Gibbs (2017) on practitioners' experiences of, and views about, remote attendance in the criminal courts, and evidence given by various individuals and organisations to the House of Commons Justice Committee (2019) about proposed extensions to video use, have underlined potential deficits to justice associated with remote hearings. The key points are summarised here.

Technical problems with establishing remote links, and maintaining good quality audio and video, are commonly reported (including during the piloting of the only full video hearings that have been independently evaluated thus far[29]). In addition to the obvious ways in which such glitches will impede ability to communicate, vulnerabilities among court users such as learning needs are thought likely to create additional challenges for communicating remotely (see Chapter Three). This includes the limited opportunities to identify vulnerability in the first instance when a party is not physically present in court. Video hearings have been deemed unsuitable for court users with additional language needs or LiPs and are said to create barriers to communication between a party and their lawyer, and also to negatively affect engagement with the court, which could influence outcome. Research on the use of secure video-links from police station to court for first hearings found that the rate of guilty pleas and custodial sentences were higher in the two pilot sites than in traditional comparator courts (Fielding et al, 2020).

Remote administration of justice is being hastily organised in response to COVID-19 (see Chapter Five) and caution about changes to the hearing procedure has arguably been set aside to ensure compliance with social distancing rules while trying to keep at least some of the show on the road. Efforts to document the issues arising, especially the experiences of lay participants in this impromptu, emergency pilot, will add to the currently limited evidence base.

Online forms and processes

Increasingly, online form–filling is the norm in many aspects of life. Susskind (2019), a strong proponent of 'online courts' and advisor on the court reform programme, argues digital processes will improve access to justice by making minor conflicts easier and less expensive to resolve, thus freeing up costly court time for more complex legal work. While noting the first iteration of online processes is largely devoted to the more straightforward work of the lower courts, including, for example, resolving small–scale civil disputes, he envisions that advances in technology could radically transform how justice is delivered. His description of these future systems seems less fantastical in light of the emergency response to COVID-19:

> All users might be visible, arrayed perhaps like participants in the TV quiz show, University Challenge … More sophisticated still would be systems that arrange all or many of those linked in a way that resembles the appearance of a court. Using immersive telepresence technologies, participants might in fact feel they are all gathered together in one place. (2019: 59)

In the here and now, there is evidence of user satisfaction with some initial online court resources.[30] However, an obvious concern is the level of access to IT and of digital literacy among court users and the impact of this upon access to justice. An independent report on digital exclusion (JUSTICE, 2018) cites research data on internet access among the general population to show that those most lacking IT access, and basic digital skills, are concentrated in more vulnerable groups – largely the same 'groups' that are over-represented among court users. Digital literacy potentially creates further challenges for those who are self-representing, particularly in the context of reduced availability of legal advice and information services. Creating an accessible online system requires careful design, including investment in developing appropriate guidance for lay users, but also enhancing public legal education more generally (Susskind, 2019). While there are various proposed mechanisms to support the use of digital resources, these are currently in planning and largely untested. The Single Justice Procedure offers online administration of justice by a single magistrate for low-level cases that would result in a financial penalty. While arguably convenient, concerns have been raised about whether online systems permit proper consideration of the consequences of pleading guilty.

Court closures

HMCTS has closed 127 courts since reforms were introduced (NAO, 2019), making it more difficult for people to attend a local court. Despite proposals to increase virtual hearings, in-person hearings will continue to be recommended for many court users with vulnerabilities and for LiPs, albeit it remains to be seen whether the responses to the COVID-19 pandemic will have a sustained impact in this regard.

HMCTS has defined as 'reasonable' a journey that involves leaving home by 7.30 am and returning no later than 7.30 pm, including a four-hour round trip on public transport. Already there is evidence for why such calculations do not translate well to real life[31] and there have been calls for the government to commission independent research into the effects of court closures on lay participants. A single local analysis of the impact of the closure of two of three courts in Suffolk (Adisa, 2018) found this had increased incidence of non-appearance of lay participants in the areas furthest from the remaining court and had disrupted informal relationships that had been built between court staff and defence advocates working on behalf of their clients. Closing ill-adapted or under-used court buildings might be less controversial if alternative 'justice spaces' were available. The law reform organisation JUSTICE recommends combining remote access with more imaginative approaches to physical venues, such as the use of 'pop-up-courts' in appropriate community venues (JUSTICE, 2019). The emphasis on staying local during the pandemic lockdown might create greater impetus in future for enhancing aspects of local infrastructure to provide this function.

Conclusion

This chapter has touched on some of the factors that influence lay participation in justice processes. It highlights to what extent and for whom the courts have been willing to adapt, and where systems and structures continue to inhibit or deny support. It notes the importance of professional competence and judicial discretion in creating cultural change to better accommodate lay users and cites current debates about the impact of court reforms on access to justice. While funds – or lack thereof – are at the forefront of much policy discussion, user experiences of the courts point also to ways in which lay participation can be better understood and professional practice duly enhanced – issues that are considered more fully in the chapters that follow.

Notes

[1] A defendant may be deemed 'unfit to plead' if he or she is considered unable to: understand charge(s); decide upon plea; be able to challenge jurors; instruct lawyers; follow proceedings; and give evidence in his or her own defence. Witness competence to give evidence at trial (s 53 of the YJCEA 1999) states the witness should be able to understand questions put to him or her and give answers that can be understood.

[2] As enshrined in Article 6 of the European Convention on Human Rights.

[3] High Court Justice in the Family Division since 2013.

[4] For example, through provision for Victim Personal Statements, special measures and separate waiting areas at court for victims/witnesses.

[5] Registered intermediaries are trained, accredited and regulated by the Ministry of Justice. Intermediaries within this scheme support two-way communication with vulnerable victims and witnesses. Some work is also undertaken in family proceedings. Non-registered RIs are not accredited, but are trained to undertake this work.

[6] No automatic eligibility for live-link for defendants under the age of 18. They must be proved to have compromised ability to participate effectively due to level of intellectual or social functioning, but also that the live-link will allow more effective participation. There is a higher threshold for adult defendants in that it is not available to defendants with physical disabilities or to intimidated defendants.

[7] First mention of 'vulnerable witness' was in 'Speaking up for justice' (Home Office, 1998), which gave rise to special measures' provisions in the YJCEA (1999).

[8] www.icca.ac.uk/further-rowith-effect-from-3-june-2019-s-28-of-the-youth-justice-and-criminal-evidence-act-1999

[9] The Human Rights Act 1998; The Disability Discrimination Act 2005; The Equality Act 2010.

[10] The Review Panel took evidence from over 700 individuals and organisations involved in family justice.

[11] The launch of a single Family Court for England and Wales was intended to set groundwork for a modernisation programme. This focused on changing the culture of the court through strong judicial governance and evidence-based practice.

[12] The Office for Standards in Education, Children's Services and Skills. Inspection of Cafcass as a national organisation (2018), available from: https://reports.ofsted.gov.uk/provider/12/1027080

[13] The exceptional case funding scheme requires evidence of domestic abuse such as a criminal conviction or civil injunction; however, this applies only to the party who has experienced abuse and not the perpetrator.

[14] www.theguardian.com/society/2018/may/30/domestic-abusers-still-able-to-cross-examine-victims-in-court; www.resolution.org.uk/news/resolution-the-law-society-and-womens-aid-issue-joint-call-to-government-to-urgently-ban-cross-examination-of-victims-by-their-abusers-in-the-family-courts/

[15] The Bill had its first reading in March 2020.

[16] https://assets.publishing.service.gov.uk/government/uploads/system/uploads/attachment_data/file/681275/guidance-courts-on-payment-certain-mmeasures-family-proceedings.pdf

[17] www.judiciary.uk/wp-content/uploads/JCO/Documents/Practice+Directions/Tribunals/Childvulnerableadultandsensitivewitnesses.pdf

[18] The Advocate's Gateway aims to promote high ethical standards when questioning people who are vulnerable in justice settings.

[19] https://assets.publishing.service.gov.uk/government/uploads/system/uploads/attachment_data/file/775594/Public_Accounts_Committee_Recommendation_2_31_Jan_2019.pdf

[20] www.gov.uk/guidance/criminal-legal-aid-means-testing#overview

[21] Includes calculating 'disposable household income', taking account of claimant's family circumstances, living costs and assets.

[22] www.gov.uk/court-fees-what-they-are

[23] www.theguardian.com/law/2019/jul/03/family-courts-running-up-a-down-escalator-due-to-increase-in-cases

[24] Interviews were conducted with ten prosecutors from the Independent Bar, seven magistrates and four District Judges, and an online survey interview was completed by 42 prosecutors.

[25] www.theguardian.com/law/2019/nov/24/legal-aid-cuts-prompt-rise-in-unrepresented-defendants

[26] Founded in 2015 to develop realistic but radical proposals with cross-party appeal for re-establishing the right to justice. The commission compiled written and oral evidence from over 100 academics and individuals working in the criminal justice system and related organisations.

[27] www.gov.uk/guidance/hmcts-reform-programme-projects-explained

[28] See Transform Justice for useful synopsis of key research and commentary: www.transformjustice.org.uk/bedtime-reading-list-on-digital-court-reform-and-court-closures/

[29] First-tier Tribunal (Tax) (Rossner and McCurdy, 2018).

[30] For example, HMCTS (2019) reports positive feedback on the online applications for divorce.

[31] www.civillitigationbrief.com/2019/05/14/court-reform-view-from-the-district-judges-we-question-whether-there-has-been-meaningful-as-opposed-to-token-consultation-with-all-levels-of-the-judiciary/

References

Adisa, O. (2018) 'Access to justice: assessing the impact of the magistrates' court closures in Suffolk', a research report, University of Suffolk.

The Bach Commission (2017) *The Right to Justice*, London: Fabian Society.

Baverstock, J. (2016) *Process Evaluation of Pre-recorded Cross-examination Pilot (s. 28)*, London: Ministry of Justice.

Blake, J. (2011) 'Current problems in asylum and protection law: the UK judicial perspective', paper presented at the Ninth World Conference of the International Association of Refugee Law Judges, 7 September, Slovenia.

Bradley, K. (2009) *The Bradley Report: Lord Bradley's Report of People with Mental Health Problems or Learning Disabilities in the CJS*, London: Department of Health.

Brown, K., Ecclestone, K. and Emmel, N. (2017) 'The many faces of vulnerability', *Social Policy and Society*, 16(3): 497–510.

Burton, M., Evans, R. and Sanders, A. (2006) *Are Special Measures for Vulnerable and Intimidated Witnesses Working? Evidence from the Criminal Justice Agencies*, London: Home Office.

Busby, N. and McDermont, M. (2012) 'Workers, marginalised voices and the employment tribunal system: some preliminary findings', *Industrial Law Journal*, 41(2): 166–83.

Charles, C. (2012) *Special Measures for Vulnerable and Intimidated Witnesses: Research Exploring the Decisions and Actions Taken by Prosecutors in a Sample of CPS Case Files*, London: Crown Prosecution Service.

Civil Justice Council (2020) *Vulnerable Witnesses in Civil Proceedings: Current Position and Recommendations for Change*, London: Civil Justice Council.

Cooper, P. (2018) 'Participation of vulnerable people: don't expect fireworks', *Family Law Journal*, 48 (Jan): 3.

Cooper, P. and Arnold, J. (2017) 'Listening without prejudice? Procedural adjustments in the employment tribunal', ELA briefing, March, 5–7.

Cooper, P., Marchant, R. and Backen, P. (2015) 'Getting to grips with ground rules hearings: a checklist for judges, advocates and intermediaries to promote the fair treatment of vulnerable people in court', *Criminal Law Review*, 6: 420–35.

Cooper, P. and Wurtzel, D. (2013) 'A day late and a dollar short: in search of an intermediary scheme for vulnerable defendants in England and Wales', *Criminal Law Review*, 1: 4–22.

Corbett, N.E. and Summerfield, A. (2017) *Alleged Perpetrators of Abuse as Litigants in Person in Private Family Law: The Cross-Examination of Intimidated and Vulnerable Witnesses*, London: Ministry of Justice.

Criminal Practice Directions I: General matters – 3D: Vulnerable People in the Courts; 3E: Ground rules hearings to plan the questioning of a vulnerable witness or defendant; 3F: Intermediaries; 3G: Vulnerable defendants.

Criminal Procedure Rules and Criminal Practice Directions, October 2015 edition, amended April 2016, especially Criminal Procedure Rules, 3.9: Case preparation and progression; 3.11: Conduct of a trial or an appeal.

Crown Prosecution Service (2016) *Speaking to Witnesses at Court: CPS Guidance*, London: CPS.

The Detention Forum (2015) 'Rethinking "vulnerability" in detention: a crisis of harm', available from: http://detentionforum.org.uk/2015/07/09/rethinking-vulnerability-in-detention-a-crisis-of-harm/

Fairclough, S. (2016) ' "It doesn't happen ... and I've never thought it was necessary for it to happen": barriers to vulnerable defendants giving evidence by live link in crown court trials', *International Journal of Evidence and Proof*, 24(8): 1–19.

Fairclough, S. (2018) 'Speaking up for injustice: reconsidering the provision of special measures through the lens of equality', *Criminal Law Review*, 1: 4–19.

Family Justice Review Panel (2011) *Family Justice Review: Final Report*, London: Ministry of Justice and Department for Education.

Fielding, N., Braun, S., Hieke, G. and Mainwaring, C. (2020) 'Video enabled justice evaluation', Sussex Police and Crime Commissioner and University of Surrey, available from: http://spccweb.thco.co.uk/media/4851/vej-final-report-ver-11b.pdf

Genn, H., Lever, B., Gray, L., Balmer, N. and National Centre for Social Research (2006) *Tribunals for Diverse Users*, DCA Research Series 1/06, London: DCA.

Gibbs, P. (2017) *Defendants on Video – Conveyor Belt Justice or Revolution of Access?*, London: Transform Justice.

Gill, N., Rotter, R., Burridge, A. and Allsopp, J. (2017) 'The limits of procedural discretion: unequal treatment and vulnerability in Britain's asylum appeals', *Social and Legal Studies*, 27(1): 49–78.

Hamlyn, B., Phelps, A., Turtle, J. and Sattar, G. (2004) *Are Special Measures Working? Evidence from Surveys of Vulnerable and Intimidated Witnesses*, London: Home Office.

Henderson, S. (2016) 'Taking control of cross-examination: judges, advocates and intermediaries discuss judicial management of the cross-examination of vulnerable people', *Criminal Law Review*, 3: 181–205.

Her Majesty's Courts and Tribunals Service (2019) 'Reform update: summer 2019', available from: https://assets.publishing.service.gov.uk/government/uploads/system/uploads/attachment_data/file/806959/HMCTS_Reform_Update_Summer_19.pdf

House of Commons Justice Committee (2015) *Inquiry into Criminal Courts Charge. Second Report of 2015/16*, London: House of Commons.

House of Commons Justice Committee (2016) *Inquiry into Courts and Tribunals Fees: Second Report of 2016/17*, London: House of Commons.

House of Commons Justice Committee (2019) *Inquiry into Courts and Tribunals Reforms: Second Report of 2019*, London: House of Commons.

Hoyano, L. and Rafferty, A. (2017) 'Rationing defence intermediaries under the April 2016 Criminal Practice Direction', *Criminal Law Review*, 2: 93–105.

Hunter, G., Jacobson, J. and Kirby, A. (2018) *Judicial Perceptions of the Quality of Criminal Advocacy*, London: Solicitors Regulation Authority and Bar Standards Board.

Jacobson, J. (2017) 'Introduction', in P. Cooper and H. Norton (eds) *Vulnerable People and the Criminal Justice System: A Guide to Law and Practice*, Oxford: Oxford University Press, pp 1–21.

Jacobson, J., Bhardwa, B., Gyateng, T., Hunter, G. and Hough, M. (2010) Punishing Disadvantage: A Profile of Children in Custody, London: Prison Reform Trust.

Jacobson, J., Hunter, G. and Kirby, A. (2015) *Inside Crown Court: Personal Experiences and Questions of Legitimacy*, Bristol: Policy Press.

Jacobson, J. and Talbot, J. (2009) *Vulnerable Defendants in the Criminal Courts: A Review of Provision for Adults and Children*, London: Prison Reform Trust.

Judicial College (2018) *Equal Treatment Bench Book: February 2018 Edition (March 2020 Revision)*, London: Judicial College.

Judicial Working Group on Litigants in Person (2013) *Judiciary of England and Wales*, available from: www.judiciary.uk/wp-content/uploads/JCO/Documents/Reports/lip_2013.pdf

Judiciary of England and Wales (2015) *Report of the Vulnerable Witnesses and Children Working Group*, available from: www.judiciary.uk/wp-content/uploads/2015/03/vwcwg-report-march-2015.pdf

JUSTICE (2018) *Preventing Digital Exclusion from Online Justice: A Report of JUSTICE*, available from: https://justice.org.uk/wp-content/uploads/2018/06/Preventing-Digital-Exclusion-from-Online-Justice.pdf

JUSTICE (2019) *Understanding Courts: A Report by JUSTICE*, London: JUSTICE, available from: https://justice.org.uk/wp-content/uploads/2019/01/Understanding-Courts.pdf

Khalifeh, H., Howard, L., Osborn D., Moran, P. and Johnson, S. (2013) 'Violence against people with disability in England and wales: findings from a National Cross-Sectional Survey', *PLoS ONE*, 8(2): e55952.

Kirby, A. (2017) 'Effectively engaging victims, witnesses and defendants in the criminal courts: a question of "court culture"?' *Criminal Law Review*, 12: 949–68.

Kirk, E., McDermont, M. and Busby, N. (2015) *Employment Tribunal Claims – Debunking the Myths*, Bristol: University of Bristol.

Law for Life (2014) 'Meeting the information needs of litigants in person', June, available from: www.lawforlife.org.uk/wp-content/uploads/Meeting-the-information-needs-of-litigants-in-person.pdf

The Law Society (2017) 'Access denied? LASPO four years on: a Law Society review', Law Society of England and Wales, available from: www.lawsociety.org.uk/support-services/research-trends/laspo-4-years-on/

Lee, R. and Tkacukova, T. (2017) 'A study of litigants in person in Birmingham Justice Centre', Birmingham: Centre for Professional Legal Education, available from: http://epapers.bham.ac.uk/3014/1/cepler_working_paper_2_2017.pdf

Legal Aid Agency (2018) 'Interests of justice: guidance on the consideration of defence representation orders', available from: https://assets.publishing.service.gov.uk/government/uploads/system/uploads/attachment_data/file/858654/Interests_of_justice_desktop_aid_2018_v2_.pdf

Leggatt, A. (2001) *Tribunals for Users: One System, One Service*, London: The Stationery Office.

Marks, A. (2016) 'What is a court? A report by JUSTICE', available from: https://justice.org.uk/wp-content/uploads/2016/05/JUSTICE-What-is-a-Court-Report-2016.pdf

McKeever, G. (2013) 'A ladder of legal participation for tribunal users', *Public Law*, 7: 575–98.

McKeever, G. (2020) 'Comparing courts and tribunals through the lens of legal participation', *Civil Justice Quarterly*, 39(3): 217–36.

McKeever, G., Royal-Dawson, L., Kirk, E. and McCord, J. (2018) *Litigants in Person in Northern Ireland: Barriers to Legal Participation*, Belfast: Ulster University.

Ministry of Justice (2010) 'Proposals for the reform of legal aid in England and Wales', available from: https://assets.publishing.service.gov.uk/government/uploads/system/uploads/attachment_data/file/228970/7967.pdf

Ministry of Justice (2011) 'Achieving best evidence in criminal proceedings: guidance on interviewing victims and witnesses, and guidance on using special measures', available from: www.cps.gov.uk/sites/default/files/documents/legal_guidance/best_evidence_in_criminal_proceedings.pdf

Ministry of Justice (2013) 'Transforming the CJS: a strategy and action plan for the criminal justice system', available from: https://assets.publishing.service.gov.uk/government/uploads/system/uploads/attachment_data/file/209659/transforming-cjs-2013.pdf

Ministry of Justice (2014) 'Report on review of ways to reduce the distress of victims in trials of sexual violence', available from: https://assets.publishing.service.gov.uk/government/uploads/system/uploads/attachment_data/file/299341/report-on-review-of-ways-to-reduce-distress-of-victims-in-trials-of-sexual-violence.pdf

Ministry of Justice (2016) 'Transforming our justice system: by the Lord Chancellor, the Lord Chief Justice and the Senior President of Tribunals', available from: https://assets.publishing.service.gov.uk/government/uploads/system/uploads/attachment_data/file/553261/joint-vision-statement.pdf

Ministry of Justice (2019a) 'The witness intermediary scheme: annual report 2018/19', available from: https://assets.publishing.service. gov.uk/government/uploads/system/uploads/attachment_data/ file/887122/witness-inter-scheme-annual-report.pdf

Ministry of Justice (2019b) 'Family Court statistics quarterly, England and Wales, July to September 2019', available from: https://assets. publishing.service.gov.uk/government/uploads/system/uploads/ attachment_data/file/857335/FCSQ_July_to_September_2019_ 2.pdf

Ministry of Justice (2019c) 'Legal support: the way ahead. An action plan to deliver better support to people experiencing legal problems', available from: https://assets.publishing.service.gov. uk/government/uploads/system/uploads/attachment_data/file/ 777036/legal-support-the-way-ahead.pdf

Moorehead, R. and Sefton, M. (2005) *Litigants in Person: Unrepresented Litigants in First Instance Proceedings*, DCA Research Series, 2/05, London: DCA.

Munby, J. (2016) Address of the President Sir James Munby at the annual dinner of the Family Law Bar Association in Middle Temple Hall on 26 February 2016.

National Audit Office (2014) 'Implementing reforms to civil legal aid', available from: www.nao.org.uk/wp-content/uploads/2014/ 11/Implementing-reforms-to-civil-legal-aid1.pdf

National Audit Office (2018) 'Early progress in transforming courts and tribunals', available from: www.nao.org.uk/wp-content/uploads/ 2018/05/Early-progess-in-transforming-courts-and-tribunals.pdf

National Audit Office (2019) 'Transforming courts and tribunals: A progress update', available from: www.nao.org.uk/wp-content/ uploads/2019/09/Transforming-Courts-and-Tribunals.pdf

Owusu-Bempah, A. (2018) 'The interpretation and application of the right to effective participation', *International Journal of Evidence and Proof*, 22(4): 321–41.

Pettit, B., Greenhead, S., Khalifeh, H., Drennan, V., Hart, J., Hogg, J., Borschmann, R., Mamo, E. and Moran, P. (2013) 'At risk yet dismissed: the criminal victimisation of people with mental health problems', available from: www.mind.org.uk/media-a/4121/at-risk-yet-dismissed-report.pdf

Plotnikoff, J. and Woolfson, R. (2007) *The 'Go-Between': Evaluation of Intermediary Pathfinder Projects*, London: Ministry of Justice.

Plotnikoff, J. and Woolfson, R. (2016) 'Worth waiting for: the benefits of section 28 pre-trial cross-examination', *Archbold Review*, 8 September, Issue 8: 6–9.

Pollert, A. (2010) 'The lived experience of isolation for vulnerable workers facing workplace grievances in 21st-century Britain', *Economic and Industrial Democracy*, 31(1): 62–92.

Pyper, D., McGuiness, F. and Brown, J. (2017) 'House of Commons Library briefing paper no. 7081: employment tribunal fees', London: House of Commons Library.

Roberts, P., Cooper, D. and Judge S. (2005) 'Monitoring success, accounting for failure: the outcome of prosecutors' applications for special measures directions under the Youth Justice and Criminal Evidence Act 1999', *International Journal of Evidence and Proof*, 9(4): 269–90.

Rossner, M. and McCurdy, M. (2018) *Implementing Video Hearings (Party-to-State): A Process Evaluation*, London: Ministry of Justice.

Royal College of Psychiatrists (2016) *Consultation Response to Immigration and Asylum Appeals on Proposals to Expedite Appeals by Immigration Detainees*, London: Royal College of Psychiatrists.

Ryder, E. (2012) 'Judicial proposals for the modernisation of Family Justice: Mr Justice Ryder', Judiciary of England and Wales, available from: www.judiciary.uk/wp-content/uploads/JCO/Documents/Reports/ryderj_recommendations_final.pdf

Shaw, S. (2016) *Review into the Welfare in Detention of Vulnerable Persons: A Report to the Home Office by Stephen Shaw*, London: HM Stationery Office.

Susskind, R. (2019) *Online Courts and the Future of Justice*, Oxford: Oxford University Press.

Thomas, R. (2013) 'From "adversarial v inquisitorial" to "active, enabling, and investigative": developments in UK', in R. Thomas, L. Jacobs and S. Baglay (eds) *The Nature of Inquisitorial Processes in Administrative Regimes: Global Perspectives*, Farnham: Ashgate Publishing, pp 51–70.

Thomson, J. and Becker, J. (2019) *Unrepresented Defendants: Perceived Effects on the Crown Court in England and Wales – Practitioners' Perspectives*, London: Ministry of Justice.

Tonry, M. (2010) 'Rebalancing the criminal justice system in favour of the victim: the costly consequences of populist rhetoric', in A. Bottoms and J. Roberts (eds) *Hearing the Victim: Adversarial Justice, Crime Victims*, Abingdon: Routledge, pp 72–103.

Transform Justice (2016) 'Justice denied? The experience of litigants in person in the criminal courts', available from: www. transformjustice.org.uk/wp-content/uploads/2016/04/TJ-APRIL_Singles.pdf

Trinder, L., Hunter, R., Hitchings, E., Miles, J., Moorhead, R., Smith, L., Sefton, M., Hinchly, V., Bader, K. and Pearce, J. (2014) *Litigants in Person on Family Law Cases*, London: Ministry of Justice.

Tribunals Judiciary (2008) 'Practice Direction First Tier and Upper Tribunal: Child, vulnerable adult and sensitive witnesses', London: Tribunals Judiciary, available from: www.judiciary.uk/ wp-content/uploads/JCO/Documents/Practice+Directions/ Tribunals/Childvulnerableadultandsensitivewitnesses.pdf

Tribunals Judiciary (2010) 'Joint Presidential Guidance Note no 2 of 2010: Child, vulnerable adult and sensitive appellant guidance', London: Tribunals Judiciary, available from: www.judiciary.uk/ wp-content/uploads/2014/07/ChildWitnessGuidance.pdf

Wheatcroft, J., Wagstaff, G. and Moran, A. (2009) 'Re-victimising the victim? How rape victims experience the UK legal system', *Victims and Offenders*, 4(3): 265–84.

Williams, K. (2011) *Litigants in Person: A Literature Review*, Research Summary, 2/11, London: Ministry of Justice.

Wurtzel, D. and Marchant, R. (2017) 'Intermediaries', in P. Cooper and H. Norton (eds) *Vulnerable People and the Criminal Justice System: A Guide to Law and Practice*, Oxford: Oxford University Press.

THREE

Conceptualising Participation: Practitioner Accounts

Amy Kirby

Introduction

This chapter and the one that follows present the findings of the empirical component of the study. This chapter focuses on the interviews conducted with 159 practitioners working in and around a number of court and tribunal settings: predominantly the criminal courts (both Crown and magistrates'), Family Court, Employment Tribunal (ET) and Immigration and Asylum Chamber (IAC). As will be discussed, the interview findings point to a range of ways in which the practitioners understood the meaning and functions of participation by lay witnesses and parties – henceforth 'court users' – in oral hearings held as part of judicial proceedings. From these accounts, it is possible to discern ten overlapping and interlinked conceptualisations of what participation entails and why it matters. The discussion here thus reflects practitioners' own definitions and understandings of participation rather than those presented in the wider policy and academic literature, which are described elsewhere in this volume.

Practitioner accounts provide insight into the meanings and functions of participation from the perspectives of those immersed in the day-to-day realities of the courts, and generate knowledge about how participation is mediated by those who directly interact with court users. This is an important undertaking as it has a bearing on how, and the extent to which, participation is achieved in practice. The final part of the chapter examines what practitioners had to say about barriers to and facilitators of participation, which advances thinking about how participation can be better supported in future.

Interviews with practitioners: rationale and methodological approach

The practitioners interviewed for the study included judges, lawyers, magistrates, court staff and others who regularly attend court and tribunal hearings in a professional capacity, or provide support to witnesses or parties attending court. The introduction to this volume briefly set out some of the ways in which participation as a legal principle is articulated in law and procedural and practice guidance. The aim of the interviews was to examine how participation, and the part it plays in the delivery of justice, is conceptualised by those who have regular contact with court users, or – in various ways – have some part to play in shaping the court environment.

Following selection of the judicial settings and three geographic sites (one Welsh and two English cities and their surrounding areas) in which the research was to be conducted (see Chapter One), formal approval for the interviews with practitioners was obtained from national bodies where required: the Judicial Office with regard to judges and magistrates; HM Courts and Tribunals Service for court staff; Cafcass (the Children and Family Court Advisory and Support Service) and Cafcass Cymru for Cafcass officers; and HM Prisons and Probation Service for probation officers.

Research access was additionally negotiated nationally and locally with relevant agencies and services. The research team adopted a purposive, convenience approach to sampling (see Bryman, 2016), whereby target numbers of respondents within each practitioner category were agreed, and recruitment was undertaken through local professional contacts and networks.[1]

In total, 159 practitioners were interviewed, the large majority of whom worked in the fields of criminal, family, employment and immigration law. A small number worked in the coronial jurisdiction, in other areas of justice or cross-jurisdictionally. The practitioners were drawn from various backgrounds, which are categorised as follows:

- Judiciary: circuit judges, district judges, magistrates, employment and tribunal judges and one coroner.
- Lawyers: solicitors and barristers across all the specified jurisdictions, some of whom were involved in pro bono services.
- Court staff: legal advisors to magistrates (in both the criminal and family jurisdictions) and ushers.
- Voluntary sector practitioners: paid staff and volunteers from a range of services working with court users, including the Witness Service, Personal Support Unit,[2] Coroners' Courts Support Service and Trade Unions.[3] Intermediaries are also included in this category.[4]
- Statutory sector practitioners: this is a broad category encompassing professionals who attend court as part of their role with statutory services such as probation, social services, Cafcass, and criminal justice liaison and diversion services. A small number of Home Office Presentation Officers (HOPOs), who represent the Home Office in IAC hearings, are included in this category.

The breakdown of respondents by jurisdiction and role is set out in Table 3.1. The interviews with this diverse range of practitioners enabled the research team to examine how participation is understood from multiple vantage points, including

Table 3.1: Breakdown of respondents by jurisdiction and role

Primary jurisdiction	Number	Percentage	Role	Number	Percentage
Crime	63	40	Judiciary	55	35
Family	46	29	Lawyer	27	17
Employment	19	12	Court staff	13	8
Immigration and Asylum	15	9	Voluntary sector	39	24
Coronial	7	4	Statutory sector	25	16
Other*	9	6			
Total	159	100	Total	159	100

* This group comprises those who had no primary jurisdiction or worked in other parts of the justice system.

those of practitioners with varying levels of interaction with, and relations to, court users. The table shows that some jurisdictions and roles were overrepresented in the sample. For example, two fifths of respondents were from the criminal jurisdiction; however, this should be seen in the context of the criminal courts having the highest volume of cases of the jurisdictions under study (see Figure 1.1 in Chapter One). The small number of respondents from the coronial jurisdiction reflects the exploratory nature of this part of the study. Members of the judiciary accounted for over one third of the sample, which can be seen as a strength of the study given that scant existing research has incorporated such a cross-section (in terms of both jurisdiction and status) of judicial perspectives on court users and participation. While the following discussion of findings draws some comparisons between jurisdictions and roles, the varying levels of representation pose limits on the extent to which this can be done.

The practitioner interviews lasted around 45 minutes on average and were conducted face-to-face or via telephone in accordance with respondents' preferences. A small number of group interviews were held, to suit the respondents' convenience, but most were one-to-one. The interviews were semi-structured and guided by an interview schedule which was oriented around three main themes: what respondents considered to be 'effective participation'; whether and on what grounds they believed participation by court users to be important; and what they perceived to be the main barriers to and (actual and potential) facilitators of participation. With respondents' permission, interviews were audio-recorded and transcribed by an external transcription company. A thematic approach to analysis of the transcripts was adopted, involving the iterative development and refinement of a coding framework structured around respondents' conceptualisations of participation and key barriers and facilitators.

What is participation?

Respondents across all jurisdictions and roles tended to speak of court users' participation in judicial proceedings as essential to the delivery of justice. In so doing, they did not draw upon ready-made or precise definitions of participation, but rather articulated the concept in a wide range of ways. Through close analysis of the interview transcripts, the research team identified several contrasting conceptualisations of what court user participation entails, and the functions of participation, as set out in Box 3.1.

I will now examine each of the six perspectives on 'what participation entails' that emerged from the data, with discussion of practitioners' perspectives on 'functions' to follow in the next section of this chapter. In advance of that, it is important to note three general points. First, what are described here as practitioners' contrasting perspectives on participation and why it matters are not clear-cut or discrete. They are, rather, closely overlapping ways of talking about participation from which the research team have identified certain key features. Secondly, respondents varied widely in terms of which, and how many, of the conceptualisations they tended to articulate in their answers to the interview questions. Thirdly, there were salient areas of both difference and similarity in these articulations between jurisdictions and roles – demonstrating that while participation must be understood as a multifaceted phenomenon, it can be usefully examined and applied cross-jurisdictionally.[5]

Box 3.1: Conceptualisations of participation

Practitioners variously described **what participation entails** in terms of:

- the provision and/or elicitation of information for the court;
- being informed about proceedings;
- having legal representation;
- protection of well-being;
- the management of the court user, such that disruption to proceedings is avoided;
- presence at proceedings.

Practitioners variously described the **functions of participation** in terms of:

- the exercise of legal rights;
- enabling court decision making;
- legitimation of court processes and outcomes;
- potential therapeutic benefits.

Participation entails: providing and eliciting information

A large majority of practitioners described participation by court users as a matter of *providing information*, by giving evidence or submitting statements to the court; or *eliciting information*, for example, by asking questions of other parties or witnesses. The 'information-provider' (see Edwards, 2004) or 'information–elicitor' role of lay participation was articulated by respondents in each practitioner group and across all the five jurisdictions. Box 3.2 provides some short examples of the numerous comments on this theme.

Some respondents spoke of participation *only* in terms of – and thus as equating to – provision of information. For example, when asked to describe what participation means, a Witness Service volunteer replied: "I assume you mean participating in the fact of giving evidence, because that's the only time they [witnesses/complainants] are participating." However, many others spoke of the provision and elicitation of information as one of several aspects of participation; for example, in most of the Box 3.2 quotations the respondents also referred to participation as a matter of being informed.[6]

Box 3.2: Providing and eliciting information

'They've got to be able to express themselves, I mean, they've got to be able to say what they want to say in a court setting. They've got to know what ... they should be saying and what documents they either should be producing, or are 'allowed' to produce.' (Judge; immigration)

'It is making sure that they can give the best evidence that they can. Because it seems to me that they need to understand, obviously, what's happening in the courtroom. But I think the main thrust is towards making sure that whatever they're there to do as a witness of fact, they can communicate that.' (Barrister; family)

'At a simple level, if someone has been involved in a road traffic accident, and they're also an important eyewitness to what occurred, the judge needs to ensure that that person gives a coherent account of what occurred. Not feeling under pressure. Not feeling obliged to answer at 100 miles an hour, etcetera.' (Judge; other)

'For a witness to be able to participate, they just need to listen and answer the questions that they're asked.' (Barrister; coroners)

'Well, to be able to participate, really, you need to be well enough to read documents, take it all in, work out how to structure your arguments and take part in asking questions of witnesses, work out who to call as witnesses and which documents to ask for.' (Judge; employment)

Participation entails: being informed

Indeed, references to court users *being informed* as a core component of participation were commonplace, and cross-cut professional and jurisdictional boundaries. While more than half of all respondents spoke in these terms, the lawyers were the most inclined to do so (maybe because they regard keeping clients informed as an essential aspect of their professional role). Respondents emphasised the importance of court users *understanding* the judicial process and outcomes – as neatly summarised by an intermediary who practised in the criminal courts:[7]

> 'The most important part of effective participation is having an understanding. That's having an understanding of the case that's against them. Having an understanding of what everybody is saying about them and what the whole trial process is. I don't feel that anybody can participate effectively if they don't have a full understanding.'

Practitioners spoke of court users' need to be informed about a number of interlinking matters, including the essential functions and nature of the justice system, and specific legal conventions and procedures:

> 'For me, [participation] really means being able to understand what's going on. I don't mean that in the most basic sense. I think in Coroners' Courts with inquests, you're talking about an inquisitorial process. There are lots of rules in the Coroner's court that lay people are not going to understand and appreciate.' (Solicitor; coroners)

Some said that fundamental to being informed is an understanding of courtroom language, which can pose particular difficulties for laypeople (as has been widely documented elsewhere[8] and will be considered also in Chapter Four):

'For a court user, they need to have a basic understanding of what's going to happen, which most people don't. They've got to be able to understand the language that's used. Basically, what's happening and how it impacts upon them, whether that's as a defendant or a witness or whoever. Because, I think, going into a court for someone who's never been in a court, is probably like going somewhere where they speak a foreign language and you don't speak that language ... It is very alien.' (Solicitor; crime)

Another necessary feature of informed participation was said to be that court users understand their own role within the judicial process, including what is expected of them and any limits to this:

'Lay clients won't always understand necessarily what they should do. For example, simple things like evidential matters. They won't necessarily know what documents or what evidence they should be collecting if they don't have a lawyer to advise them on that. Then, although they may actually in practice go to court and be in the hearing, they're not really participating effectively if they aren't aware of what they should be putting before the court.' (Barrister; immigration)

Participation entails: being represented

A sizeable minority of respondents – more than one quarter – closely associated court user participation with *legal representation*. For example, when asked to describe what participation means, an usher in the criminal courts responded: "I think, a lot of the time, especially with criminal cases, [participation] will be through the representative, rather than through the defendant." For these respondents, participation is problematic only where a party is unrepresented (or, perhaps, represented poorly); conversely, a party who is represented is, by definition, deemed to participate, even if they are doing so indirectly via their lawyer.[9]

As discussed in Chapter Two, access to publicly funded legal representation varies widely depending on the type of case and lay party concerned. In line with this, it was possible to discern notable differences between jurisdictions in the extent to which practitioners associated participation with representation. Most notably, those practising in the ET – where legal representation is relatively uncommon – were less inclined to speak in these terms than practitioners from other jurisdictions:

'Well it's still the case that the vast majority of defendants are represented ... Principally, you are relying upon their representative to have explained procedures, processes ... As I say, because most people are represented, you are really focusing on their representative rather than on the defendant themselves.' (Judge; crime)

'[Court users] have to tell me their story. And, it is my job to make sure they can ... It's much easier if they've got legal representation.' (Judge; immigration)

'Without the benefit of having a legal advocate, I see parents floundering in court proceedings, not understanding the very basics of even attending at court.' (Cafcass officer; family)

That the relationship between representation and participation is not entirely straightforward was alluded to by several practitioners, who pointed to the possibility that an advocate (or supporter) can get in the way of a party's active engagement with proceedings. A probation officer commented: "[Defendants] don't really get much to participate in actual court unless they're *not* represented. Everything that they do at court tends to be via the intermediary or a solicitor."

Participation entails: being protected

Around a quarter of respondents, including representatives from all jurisdictions, spoke of participation as being dependent upon the *protection of the court user's well-being*. From this perspective, court users can participate effectively only if they feel safe and reasonably comfortable within the court environment and are protected from intimidation or excessive fear or distress. A legal advisor in the criminal courts described participation in the following terms:

> 'getting the best quality evidence and experience from that particular witness, to present their best before the court, unhindered by, maybe, being too stressed, for example ... I think the court should do its utmost to try and make it more palatable for people to come to court and give off their best.'

Some respondents were concerned with the impact on court users of the formalities of the court environment or the (usually) adversarial nature of proceedings. Others, speaking mostly about victims and witnesses in the criminal courts, or parties in the Family Court, spoke more about court users' needs for protection from fear or intimidation. Also under the general theme of 'protection' were comments made about the importance of understanding and addressing court users' physical, intellectual or mental health needs which have a bearing on their participation. In light of this, practitioners spoke frequently about adjustments to the court process (see Chapter Two for more detail on these) which can help lay users to participate in a protected manner:

> 'We, as a bench ... [need to] make sure that [witnesses] aren't put under pressure with the questioning from either the defence advocate, or, indeed, the defendant put [under] undue pressure by repeated questioning from the prosecution.' (Magistrate; crime)

'It's important that [lay parties] do participate, and it's important that the court makes whatever arrangements are necessary in order to enable them to do so. That goes for people with mental health difficulties, as well as the ordinary man in the street.' (Judge; family)

Importantly, a number of practitioners argued that 'being protected' in some instances requires that the party or other individual does *not* participate in proceedings, particularly when it comes to children who are the subject of Family Court proceedings. Such children may sometimes meet the judge presiding over their case in chambers, but direct participation in proceedings was said to be rare, on the grounds that it is potentially harmful. Speaking about the potential role of the child where there are allegations of abuse, a Cafcass officer said:

'By and large, it'd be emotionally quite damaging for the child to give evidence ... It depends what other evidence the judge has against the potential perpetrator, and the after effect, the impact, that it would have on the child in terms of family relations; whether the child can emotionally deal with the magnitude of giving evidence against the perpetrator. So yes, there is an option there, but it's carefully considered.'

Participation entails: being managed

Some respondents conceived participation as something to be *managed* by practitioners so as to avoid disruption of the court process or otherwise inappropriate behaviour. Participation was spoken of in these terms by around one fifth of respondents – largely court staff and members of the judiciary, perhaps reflecting the fact that they hold primary responsibility for ensuring the smooth running of proceedings. Underlying the notion that lay participation necessitates management were some concerns about possible 'over-participation' by court users who may be inclined to provide too much, or inappropriate, information:

> 'I think it's then more about how lay people are handled. For instance, to be told in advance that they should answer the questions put to them, and even though they might have other things that they know, to be told that [these things] aren't necessarily relevant, would help.' (Magistrate; crime)

> 'I do feel [that participation is] very important, but I think the court users' understanding of participating is not necessarily the same as the tribunal's understanding, because they're not legally trained. They don't necessarily focus on relevant issues, they simply want to tell you everything. Sometimes, it's not necessary.' (Judge; immigration)

As the preceding quotations illustrate, 'over-participation' was often deemed to be borne out of a lack of understanding of the court process. Accordingly, the need for 'managed' participation was sometimes referred to in discussions of litigants in person (LiPs). Management of court users for the sake of saving court time was another issue raised, as by a magistrate in the criminal courts: 'There's always this balance between people feeling they've had a fair hearing and it needing to be managed ... especially because these days we are generally quite short of time.' Other practitioners spoke of the need to contain the heightened emotions that are often an inherent feature of involvement in judicial proceedings:

> 'They want to participate and sometimes the only difficulty is to make sure to keep them on the point, because they can get very emotional.' (Judge; other)

'I've also sat in one [hearing] where people have been kicking off, and a coroner has actually had to say, "Look, I've got two police officers here, giving evidence. I've got no qualms in getting you removed from my court." It's a balance, I think.' (Support service; coroners)

Understandings of participation as something to be managed were often expressed with reference to court users whose participation is 'obligatory' (see Owusu-Bempah, 2017) rather than voluntarily entered into, such as defendants in the criminal courts. This was also the case with regard to the final conceptualisation of what participation entails: namely, that it is about presence.

Participation entails: being present

Participation was described by a minority of practitioners as essentially a matter of *being present* at the court or tribunal hearing:

'If they don't [participate the case] will be heard in their absence and it would more likely go against them than for them. It's in their benefit to participate with the court.' (Court usher; crime)

'To actually be able to get there in terms of actually being able to access the building for whatever reasons, and also being able to get there in terms of that their needs are being met ... So it's actually being able to be there and be part of it.' (Intermediary; family)

'It's still important for them to physically be in court and see what is happening, and understand what is happening ... In fact, you participate by turning up.' (Barrister; immigration)

If not made explicit (as in the last of the previous quotations), most comments about presence implied that this should be physical rather than via remote means such as video-link. Some respondents conceived of a court user's presence as having an active dimension – on the basis that attendance at a hearing enables the individual to provide information to the court or be otherwise directly involved in proceedings. There is thus an overlap with the other understandings of participation as discussed earlier. For example, when describing what participation means, a family solicitor commented:

'[If] they're not present at the hearing, they don't participate effectively … If they're there, you can always gain instructions from them … The problem arises when they don't engage with you before the hearing or after the hearing, because then that puts you on the back foot at the hearing. Or, if they've completely disengaged with you and they don't turn up at the hearing, they can't participate at all.'

Other comments focused on passive or minimal participation through presence, with reference to circumstances in which a court user is legally obliged to attend proceedings:

'Defendants don't have any choice than to engage in the judicial role because they are the people on trial for alleged criminal offences. So when you say to what extent they should engage, if they plead guilty then they've engaged to the extent that they're going to be sentenced.' (Legal advisor; crime)

'Participation is almost a strange term to use because … the legal process is not about, if you like, bringing people together in some form of communicative exercise … To some extent the participants, many of them, may be unwilling participants, but they are essential and some of them have no choice. For example, the defendant has no choice ... He's compelled. Witnesses are summonsed.' (Witness Service; crime)

In comments such as those just quoted, the meaning of participation was articulated in a weak sense: in terms of *mere* presence or legal obligation. Notions of the 'managed' court user likewise tend to imply a weaker form of participation than most perceptions of the participating court user as one who provides or elicits information, or is informed, represented or protected. This highlights how practitioners' conceptions of participation may influence the extent to which participation is achieved in practice.

Why does participation matter?

This section of the chapter focuses on respondents' understandings of the *functions* of participation. As noted earlier, there were four main aspects to this. First, respondents spoke of participation as being, in and of itself, the exercise of one's legal rights; secondly, they described it as that which enables the court to make its decisions; thirdly, participation was said to have the function of legitimating the judicial process and outcomes; and, finally, there were references to the potential therapeutic value of participation. While the first of these understandings is of participation as an end in itself, the other three conceive of participation as having an instrumental value: that it is the means to achieving certain ends. These ends were understood to be, respectively, decision making, legitimacy and therapeutic benefits to the court user.

Participation is the exercise of legal rights

More than half of the respondents across jurisdictions and professional groups spoke of the act of participation in terms of the exercise of legal rights, including the right to a fair trial:

'[Participation] is a fundamental principle of our justice, isn't it? I know we've got human rights legislation in place, but I think that any person who is facing a crime has their absolute right to be heard and participate in that hearing.' (Legal advisor; crime)

Correspondingly, participation was said to imbue the court process with what some described as 'fairness':

'[Participation] is essential, absolutely essential, yes. It goes to the basic tenet of justice must be seen to be done. If you're made aware that someone doesn't have the ability to follow the proceedings, whether it be because they don't speak the language, whether they have some disability, whether they have a lack of ability to concentrate on matters or understand matters, then all those factors need to be taken into consideration in order to ensure that they have a fair trial ... under Article 6 of the European Convention of Human Rights.' (Judge; family)

As this quotation indicates, the notion that participation ensures a fair hearing also encompasses ideas about 'equality of arms'. This was frequently commented upon with reference to the disadvantages faced by court users arising from such factors as language difficulties, emotional or mental health needs, or absence of legal representation. This was seen as especially pertinent in the context of the IAC, where appellants are challenging the state (and with potentially life or death consequences):

'Where you have court proceedings where one side is always the government, the government comes to proceedings fully armed, or is capable of coming to the proceedings fully armed ... So we have to do our best to make sure that there's an equality of arms within court proceedings. Where one side has that built in advantage, it does mean that it is the other side that you're looking after, but doing so in a neutral way … It's very important they're able to participate because without the participation, they don't have the chance to present their [case].' (Judge; immigration)

Although respondents often spoke passionately of participation as the exercise of legal rights, several also referred to the need to manage the lay user's expectations of what this entails. For example, they referred to the problems that can arise when a court user equates exercising their legal rights with achieving their desired outcome:

'The British justice system is not a search for the truth. That's not what it is, that's never been what it's about … It's, "Have we got enough evidence to convict this person?" That's what it is and that's a very different thing. People generally think it's a search for the truth. They come and say that. I think they're disappointed by that.' (Solicitor; crime)

'The old phrase: "I want my day in court." Why? was always my question. Why? What do you think you're really going to achieve? From your point of view, from anybody else's point of view, do you really want to put yourself through that? And how will you feel if it doesn't go the way you want it to?' (Support service; family)

Participation enables decision making

Many respondents spoke of participation as having the essential function of allowing the judicial process to reach an outcome:

'The whole system will not work unless all the parties are participating and fulfilling their role properly … I don't think you're going to get justice if they're not. Quite simply. Because if you can't get witnesses into court and get them understanding what's going on, you've got nobody to give evidence; if a defendant isn't participating, he may, for example, plead not guilty when he should be pleading guilty ... or the person may plead guilty when he's not guilty.' (Judge; crime)

As described in the previous section, most practitioners conceived of participation in terms of (among other things) the provision and elicitation of information. Comments on this theme often included references to the court's need for the information in order to do its essential work of decision making:

'The question, I suppose, you pose to yourself, as a judge, in any particular case is, "What's going to help these parties give their best evidence so that you can reach the best decision and they can leave more confident that what they've experienced is justice?"' (Judge; employment)

'I think it's important that [lay participants] are as engaged as they can be. As the professionals ... We want to hear what they've got to say. We want them to give their best evidence. Particularly with family cases, we want to make sure that we've got all of the available information, so that the right decisions are being made in relation to the child who's at the centre of it.' (Legal advisor; family)

Decision making was said to be facilitated through participation by which court users were able to demonstrate their credibility or individuality. In this sense, participation was understood to have a 'humanising' quality. This was said to involve, for example, a jury being able to see and hear the testimony of witnesses before determining the verdict, a judge being able to directly interact with a litigant or defendant before reaching a decision or a legal practitioner meeting a child subject to

Family Court proceedings before representing their interests. Direct interaction with court users was said to be central to this:

'I'm always surprised and taken aback by the number of cases that I will read on paper, and then when I actually get people into court and I hear them give evidence, my impression of them, my view of the case, can completely change. You need oral evidence and you need to put people in the best position to give it. If there is any view that this can become a paper exercise, that we can get rid of the adversarial system, I'm afraid I'm completely against that. My experience is that you've got to hear the evidence.' (Judge; family)

'[Early in my judicial career], I sat with a judge, and one of the first things he told me about sentencing was: "Never send anybody to prison unless you can look them in the eye when you do it." It was a salutary lesson, and of course it's not very easy to look someone in the eye on a video link. I understand all the cost pressures, and all the rest of it, but in my view he or she should be in court, where you see them and they see you.' (Judge; other)

The last respondent quoted was not alone in raising concerns about the implications for participation (and thereby for court decision making) of the use of video-link technology; others, however, had contrasting views on remote attendance, as will be further discussed later.

Participation legitimates the judicial process and outcomes

Legitimacy is a complex and contested concept; however, broadly speaking, prominent scholars on the subject[10] argue that in order for institutions to make and maintain a 'valid' claim to hold authority (see Bottoms and Tankebe, 2012), they need to be perceived as legitimate in the eyes of the citizens that they serve. This is conceived both in terms of the presence of shared normative standards, or beliefs, between the authority and individual citizen *and* the extent to which the individual expresses consent for the authority – for example, by cooperating with it. Although they did not speak explicitly in these terms, almost half the respondents – and particularly members of the judiciary and court staff – indicated that they associated participation by court users with the users' perceptions of the court's authority as legitimate:

> '[Participation] makes all the difference in the world. You have court users participating, walking away from the court believing the case has been heard fairly whether they're the defendant or whether they're the participants in family cases. It's very, very necessary that people have an understanding and a belief they've had their chance in court to either present the case, to defend the case or to simply explain why the situation has arisen.' (Magistrate; crime)

Many respondents loosely articulated the principles of procedural justice theory, whereby 'procedurally just' treatment of court users helps to secure legitimacy.[11] Tyler (2007) identified four aspects to procedural justice in a court setting: having a voice in the process; neutrality in decision making; respectful treatment; and trust. In particular, the importance of the court user's voice within (the legal constraints of) the system was emphasised by a number of respondents, including a criminal solicitor: "Being able to participate is what makes it inherently fair because you've had your turn, you've had your voice heard, you've had fair play." Crucially, it was also said that what matters to court users is not simply that they have a voice, but that their voice is *listened to* by those administering justice:

> 'I think participation means being able to participate in every sense of the word and *feel* that you've had the

opportunity to do that as well ... Everybody needs to have the opportunity to feel that they've been listened to. That's the fairness of it, and because the decisions that are made are so important to people's lives and the children's lives.' (Solicitor; family)

Some respondents placed special weight on respectful treatment, such as an employment judge who referred to: "A bit of dialogue, a calmness of manner, measured tone, courtesy, offering breaks, that's all part of fairness. It's a process." This he described as "procedural fairness", which he distinguished from "just a substantive fairness". Others emphasised the importance of fair and equal treatment and, in line with procedural justice theory, suggested that perceptions of a fair *process* can even outweigh considerations of outcome:

'Issues like equal treatment should be as important if not more important, frankly, than getting it right because that really deals with how, when somebody leaves the courtroom, they should feel that they've had a fair hearing. There should be no doubt in their mind that everything they wanted to say has been said. They shouldn't have been cut off. They shouldn't feel as though their evidence has been curtailed unfairly, that they've been bullied or cajoled.' (Judge; immigration)

'I think in the employment tribunals, to show that people have participated effectively, we want the two people walking away to feel like ... they've been heard, and that whatever the outcome, they can accept it because they were able to fully participate in that process.' (Solicitor; employment)

Where the process is not perceived as fair, it was also suggested, an individual might be less inclined to comply or engage with the legal system in future:

'If [court users] didn't feel that their contribution was listened to and welcomed, they wouldn't be willing to repeat the experience if they were involved in another case ... If somebody has something that they feel is relevant and might make a difference to the final outcome but their voice isn't heard or their thoughts are not represented in any way, then that again could lead to frustration and, perhaps more importantly, a lack of faith in the court system.' (Magistrate; crime)

The impact that perceptions of legitimacy can have on future cooperation and compliance with authorities has been a central concern of legitimacy scholars, who argue that those with a strong belief in the legitimacy of authorities and institutions are more likely to cooperate or comply with authorities in any future interactions (Tyler, 2007).

Participation provides (potential) therapeutic benefits

It has been shown that some respondents deemed participation to have a legitimating function, in that they assumed that the effectively participating court user was more likely to view the court process and outcome as fair. Closely overlapping with this perspective is the assumption that the court user who participates effectively (also) stands to benefit *as an individual*: that, in other words, participation potentially has therapeutic benefits. In the context of the legal system, 'therapeutic' can be understood to mean interactions that contribute to the court user's well-being or are rehabilitative. As with 'legitimacy', respondents did not explicitly talk of 'therapeutic' functions, but a small number did speak in broad terms about individuals feeling 'empowered' or otherwise benefiting from participation:

'[Lay users] have to participate because otherwise it's very disempowering. They have to be part of it, they can't be, sort of, dished out things.' (Judge; immigration)

'It's not the pieces of paper that make this scenario work, it's the users themselves. So we are only providers of the tools, or the supports, to try and make that happen in as amicable a way as possible, but we are not the final resolution of the matter, because we will end; they will go on and they'd have to keep dealing with that issue.' (Legal advisor; family)

Such perspectives accord with 'therapeutic jurisprudence' models of justice, which are concerned with the consequences for well-being of involvement in formal legal processes (see, for example, Wexler, 2000). Reflecting, in part, an emphasis in both on the importance of the individual's 'voice' in judicial proceedings, there is a clear complementarity between procedural justice theory and therapeutic justice approaches (Kaiser and Holtfreter, 2016). The latter, however, are often focused on particular types of court or groups of court users.[12] In this study, the therapeutic benefits of participation were sometimes discussed in general terms, regardless of jurisdiction or the nature of the individual's role in proceedings; at other times, they were spoken of in relation to specific lay users or types of hearing. For example, it was suggested that a sentencing court's consideration of a Victim Personal Statement[13] provides for a form of participation that is therapeutic for victims of crime:

'For the complainant it's a step towards feeling, "I'm in charge on this occasion. I've been able to do it" ... Especially if they've been the subject [of] sexual abuse, it gives them some closure, it gives them a sense of empowerment that they've actually been able to tell the [defendant] to their face what it's meant to them. I think it's very important from their point of view.' (Judge; crime)

The potentially therapeutic benefits of participation were also described with reference to convicted offenders who, post-sentence, are required to report back periodically to the court on their progress on drug treatment:

> 'It's really good to see how the magistrates – and they enjoy it – interact with the defendant at the same level. Some of the defendants will say "It's the first time I've ever been given any positive feedback, ever." To receive it from an authority figure is quite powerful, so encouraging participation in that way, I think, is really good.' (Legal advisor; crime)

Barriers to and facilitators of participation

In addition to exploring practitioners' understandings of participation as a concept, the research interviews probed respondents' views on barriers to, and facilitators of, participation. The respondents often spoke at length and in detail about the range of intersecting factors that can limit participation, several of which were alluded to in the quotations set out in the preceding discussion. Many of the barriers identified by respondents have been examined in prior research (see Chapter Two), and were noted also through the observational research (to be reported in Chapter Four) – and will therefore not be examined in detail here.

In brief, however, the barriers to participation described by practitioners fell into three broad categories. The first of these were barriers said to arise from court users' needs and vulnerabilities – including mental health problems, learning disabilities and communication needs, language barriers – and other associated forms of social disadvantage or cultural difference. Secondly, respondents spoke about what might be termed the 'old' barriers to participation: long-standing structural and cultural features of the justice system which impede court users' engagement with it – such as its intimidating formality and architectural design,[14] the complexities of legal language and processes,[15] legal constraints on participation and limits to 'story-telling',[16] and endemic delays and inefficiencies.[17] Thirdly, respondents referenced what can be characterised as 'new' barriers to participation: that is, factors impacting court users which arise from recent policy developments. As described in detail in Chapter Two, these include reduced public funding for legal representation, which has led to increased numbers of LiPs across much of the justice system, and reforms introduced under the HMCTS courts modernisation programme.[18] In relation to the latter, many respondents had particular concerns about LiPs and some spoke at length about the large-scale court closures which have been seen in recent years. A related development under the courts modernisation programme is the expansion in use of remote methods of court attendance, particularly video-link. Since the time that the interviews took place, the COVID-19 pandemic has vastly (and unexpectedly) accelerated this development – in light of which, it is interesting to look in a little more depth at respondents' comments on this theme.

Remote court attendance

Respondents had mixed and often nuanced views on the value and limits of virtual or remote participation. Their reservations tended to centre around two main issues. First, there were concerns about the perceived loss of interaction and the potential impact on participation. Some referred to the absence of body language, non-verbal cues or "human cues" (judge; employment) in video-enabled or telephone hearings; others commented that remote hearings prevented practitioners appreciating the "full picture" (magistrate; crime) of the case or individual concerned. Some alluded to the risk that court users may not be able to understand or fully engage with hearings attended remotely, which was said to be a particular issue for individuals with additional needs, such as those lacking literacy or technological skills, unrepresented parties, or those receiving the assistance of an interpreter. Court user participation via video-link was sometimes described as highly constrained – such as in circumstances when the audio is muted because the court user is perceived to be disruptive (a clear illustration of 'managed' participation), or when the court user appearing by video-link is "present in the hearing but not [participating]" (barrister; crime).

A second set of reservations concerned the practical difficulties involved in video-enabled or other forms of remote participation. Those with experience of using video technology described a number of "glitches" (magistrate; crime), such as difficulties connecting, problems with sound quality and not all parties being present at the allotted time. Others raised concerns about maintaining a secure connection or the potential impact on confidentiality, such as when video consultations between defendants in custody and lawyers take place while a prison officer is sitting in the video-link room. A range of participatory and practical considerations led one immigration judge to comment:

> 'I spend a long time and put a lot of effort into making people be as at ease as they can ... It can be small bits of your body language that helps them feel at ease. I take pride, I take professional pride in letting people give their best evidence. You cannot do that over a screen. You cannot. Humanity is required to let people give their best evidence and you cannot do that over the screen ... Quite apart from the fact that I don't believe it'll ever work ... I just don't believe that the technology this side of five years is going to be good enough.'

However, positive comments were also made about remote hearings. Some respondents said that such hearings *enable* participation by court users who are otherwise unable, or would find it extremely difficult, to participate. There was support for the use of video-link as a special measure for vulnerable or intimidated court users, which facilitates 'protected' participation. An intermediary with experience of practising in the criminal courts described her experience of helping a defendant on the autism spectrum give evidence:

'He struggled to speak in front of multiple people, and he also found it difficult to give eye contact … I supported the recommendation that he should leave the courtroom and go and give evidence via live link, because basically the difference was he [otherwise] couldn't do it. He felt like he could not do it if he had to do it in a courtroom, sitting in the witness box, but he felt like he could do it if it was over video link and I was sat next to him.'

A small number of respondents commented that video-enabled participation helps to create a less formal environment in which direct interaction between practitioners and court users is made easier. The use of remote hearings was also spoken of positively in cases in which court users would have to travel very long distances, including from abroad, to give evidence or for those with medical conditions which make travel to court difficult. Remote attendance was said to be of value in "simple and straightforward" (judge; employment) cases, such as bail or case management hearings. For example, reference was made to regular use of telephone hearings for preliminary matters in the ET, and several criminal practitioners said that remote attendance from prison is useful when defendants might otherwise have to travel long distances to court in a prison van, or risk losing their current cell to another incoming prisoner.

Practitioners as facilitators

Perhaps one of the most salient findings from this study is that, when respondents were asked about how the participation of court users can be facilitated, they often spoke about the part that they themselves or other practitioners have to play in this. In other words, assisting or supporting participation – to the extent that this is possible, within the various constraints referred to earlier – was seen by many to be central to the role of practitioners in the courtroom. (The other main source of support for participation was said to be the availability of special measures or adjustments for vulnerable court users, as discussed elsewhere in this volume, which were widely described in positive terms.)

This focus on facilitating participation was evident not only in comments from respondents in explicit support roles, such as intermediaries and representatives of agencies such as the Witness Service and Cafcass. Many other practitioners, including court staff and members of the judiciary, appeared to regard the provision of assistance with participation as integral to their work:

'I will, if appropriate, give a little chat to a witness and say, 'Look, this is what's going to happen. This is what cross-examination is. It's not going to be a punch-up. It's not like TV.' All of that, again, just to settle them down …There's an awful lot that's probably going on in the back of my brain thinking about, "How can I just ensure that this person has the best opportunity to do whatever they're here to do?"' (Judge; employment)

'I always check what clients are aware of, and what they aren't aware of. If there are any gaps in that information, I try and fill that gap, and to make them feel comfortable about that because if they're unaware, or uncertain, or have difficulty understanding what's going on, that clearly means that they don't feel comfortable doing it.' (Barrister; immigration)

There may have been an element of 'interviewer effect' (see Bryman, 2016) in respondents' descriptions of their own endeavours to support court user participation. However, many spoke not only of the assistance they provide, but also that offered by their peers, and of how practitioners work together to support participation:

> 'Our clerks are very professional and friendly with the people that they encounter. We try and keep it as friendly as possible ... We don't always manage it, but we try and write [our judgments] in accessible English, not like a Chancery pleading out of Dickens ... That level of courtesy, I would hope, is not unique to us by any stretch. I think that's something you should do in all first-instance courts and tribunals.' (Judge; employment)

> 'I had a gentleman that was elderly and hard of hearing, so again, I would have addressed that with the solicitors, who then raised it with the bench, who then accepted that the individual wouldn't have to stay standing and made sure that things were fully explained during that process. The solicitor was able to turn around and explain what was happening.' (Liaison and diversion worker; crime)

Several respondents, including legal advisors themselves, said that providing help to LiPs was an important part of the legal advisor role, especially with the growth in numbers of unrepresented parties in the courts. This was described by one magistrate in the criminal courts as a "positive duty" of the role, and in the following manner by another respondent:

> 'If they're not offered the duty solicitor or it doesn't fall within the ambit of the scheme, then the legal advisors will ultimately explain to them what the procedure is. I know that lots of legal advisors ... will explain, "Well it's not my job to tell you to plead guilty or not guilty, but if I explain the law and procedure to you, you can

make your own decision on it" … It's changed our roles significantly, I think, because you're more involved with [LiPs].' (Legal advisor; family)

Some practitioners were said to go "over and above" (magistrate; crime) or "out of their way" (solicitor; employment) in their efforts to facilitate participation and to act as a bridge between an otherwise complex, intimidating system and the individual appearing within it:

'I can spend as much time with [bereaved family members] as I like. That will be around explaining what the court is about, having advice sheets for them … meeting them, talking over what the purpose is, talking about their role in helping the coroner, so that they feel as comfortable as possible when it comes to actually being physically in the court. I think there's a lot of information available, but there's a lot of human contact as well.' (Solicitor; coroners)

It was also suggested that the emphasis on inclusion and supporting court users is something of a recent trend. A judge in the criminal courts commented, "We've tended to have gone from the aloof, stuffy sort of judge approach to a more inclusive approach, a more sort of user-friendly approach, if you like," while a trade union representative (with experience of the ET) said:

'A few years back there would have been some judges who were a little old fashioned, is a polite way to put it, [laughter] and yes, maybe not quite as sensitive to diversity issues as they might have been. Genuinely, I think that's changed. There's been a lot of training put in for the tribunals, for judges and lay members, to make sure that people are aware.'

The efforts made to bridge the, sometimes substantial, gap between the system and individual court users are evidently not without personal cost to the practitioners. In interview, respondents were asked if their or their colleagues' well-being was affected by their work. In response, many spoke of the impact on themselves or their peers of the most serious or distressing cases, and particularly of hearing evidence about physical or sexual abuse or other trauma:[19]

'I know that there is a fear, and there is some evidence, that some judges who have had a constant diet of very serious sexual offences cases have felt that it has affected them psychologically and have had to take time off work.' (Judge; crime)

'If you are dealing with and speaking to people who have been through significant trauma, I mean you're speaking to people sometimes who are describing details of torture and it's very severe ... I'm not a psychologist, but I imagine it is going to affect people.' (Barrister; immigration)

Respondents also spoke of the impact of other aspects of their role, and interactions with lay users, on their well-being. Some referred to the emotional or psychological repercussions – particularly for members of the judiciary – of making life-changing decisions about individuals. There was also discussion of difficult working conditions within the courts and tribunals, associated with high caseloads or regular interaction with highly distressed or agitated court users:

'Particularly in care cases when you've had maybe a protracted hearing: you've had parents who've got their own vulnerabilities but that, sadly, aren't able to provide good enough parenting. So you're then looking at a decision to remove that child permanently from their care.

That's an enormous decision for magistrates and one which does affect them and does affect the legal advisor giving that advice, I think. It's always countered by the fact that that is the job that you signed up for and the job that you have to do. I think it would be wrong to say that it has no effect on you.' (Legal advisor; family)

'In the cases I deal with, because of the pressure on funding, I very, very rarely have a solicitor with me at court ... So, not only do I have to deal with the legal arguments and the court and everything else, but I'm also having to do all the hand-holding with the clients, which can be incredibly stressful. I had a case ... where I found [my client] huddled in a corner, in enormous distress after he'd given evidence. I had to call a halt to proceedings, and I had to get someone from my solicitors' office to come down and help take him to a psychiatric hospital ... Obviously you go home from work, and you can't just forget about that.' (Barrister; employment)

Conclusion

This chapter has examined how court user participation is understood by practitioners immersed in the 'social world' (see Rock, 1993) of courts and tribunals. The study findings point to the multifaceted nature of participation. Participation was variously said to be a matter of providing and eliciting information for the court; being informed; being legally represented; being protected; being managed; and being present. Its functions were described in terms of the exercise of legal rights; enabling court decision making; legitimation of court processes and outcomes; and potential therapeutic benefits. Practitioners' conceptualisations of what participation entails, and why it matters, are interlinked and overlapping. An important finding of this research is that participation was described in similar terms, albeit to various degrees, by respondents in different professional groups and from different jurisdictions – demonstrating the value of adopting a cross-jurisdictional approach to researching this phenomenon and considering the policy implications. This chapter has highlighted the various barriers, both 'old' and 'new', to participation and has shown that its facilitation is widely regarded as integral to the role of practitioners in the courtroom. Nevertheless, as will be illustrated in the chapter that follows, there appears to be a gap between practitioners' understandings of participation and its empirical realities.

Notes

[1] Additional assistance with recruitment was provided by a steering group and judicial reference group established for the project, and – with regard to the fieldwork conducted in Wales – by the Commission on Justice in Wales, which was set up by the Welsh Government and was undertaking a review of the justice system in Wales (2019) which coincided with the fieldwork for this project.

[2] Since the time of the research, the Personal Support Unit, which provides assistance to litigants-in-person, has been renamed Support Through Court.

[3] Specifically, trade union officials with experience of supporting ET claimants.

[4] Intermediaries facilitate communication in court, whether on a statutory basis (acting as Registered Intermediaries for witnesses in criminal cases) or as part of a non-statutory service (assisting defendants in criminal cases or parties or witnesses in the Family Court).

[5] For an analysis of the conceptual distinction between courts and tribunals through the lens of participation, see McKeever (2020). In this article, McKeever argues that, contrary to the assumption that tribunals are more likely to be participatory than the courts, there exists a spectrum of adjudication whereby some courts and tribunals are more participatory than others.

[6] This corresponds with Kirby's (2019) conceptualisation of participation as concerning the degree to which a lay user understands and expresses themselves within proceedings.

[7] In all instances where a respondent practised in more than one jurisdiction, as was the case for this interviewee, only the primary jurisdiction is referenced.

[8] See, for example, Jacobson et al (2015), JUSTICE (2019) and McKeever (2020).

[9] For a critical analysis of the extent to which legal representation acts as a 'proxy' form of participation, see Owusu-Bempah (2018). Similarly, McKeever (2020) describes the ways in which representation can both facilitate, and act as a barrier to, participation.

[10] Such as Beetham (1991) and Jackson et al (2015).

[11] And corresponding with McKeever's assertion that 'participation is an intrinsic part of procedural justice' (2020).

[12] For example, therapeutic jurisprudence has informed the development of specialist courts such as drug or domestic violence courts (Bowen and Whitehead, 2016), and has influenced developments in coroners' courts in some jurisdictions (Freckelton, 2007).

[13] A Victim Personal Statement is a victim's account of how they have been affected by the offence; where the offender is convicted, the statement may be read out in court at the sentencing hearing – sometimes by the victim themselves (www.gov.uk/government/publications/victim-personal-statement).

[14] See, for example, Carlen (1976), Mulcahy (2013), Kirby (2017) and Mulcahy and Rowden (2019).

[15] See, for example, Jacobson et al (2015), JUSTICE (2019) and McKeever (2020).

[16] See, for example, Rock (1993), Fielding (2006) and Jacobson et al (2015).

[17] See, for example, Church (1982), Duff and Leverick (2002) and Jacobson et al (2015).

[18] See, for example, National Audit Office (2014), Law Society (2017), Ministry of Justice (2018), National Audit Office (2018) and Ministry of Justice (2019).

[19] For a recent review of the impact of 'vicarious' or 'secondary trauma' on practitioner well-being, see James (2020).

References

Beetham, D. (1991) *The Legitimation of Power* (1st edn), Basingstoke: Palgrave Macmillan.

Bottoms, A. and Tankebe, J. (2012) 'Beyond procedural justice: a dialogic approach to legitimacy in criminal justice', *Journal of Criminal Law and Criminology*, 102(1): 119–70.

Bowen, P. and Whitehead, S. (2016) *Problem-Solving Courts: An Evidence Review*, London: Centre for Justice Innovation.

Bryman, A. (2016) *Social Research Methods* (5th edn), Oxford: Oxford University Press.

Carlen, P. (1976) *Magistrates' Justice*, London: Martin Robertson.

Church, T.W., Jr (1982) 'The "old and the new" conventional wisdom of court delay', *Justice System Journal*, 7(3): 395–412.

The Commission on Justice in Wales (2019) *Justice in Wales for the People of Wales Report*, Cardiff: The Commission on Justice in Wales.

Duff, P. and Leverick, F. (2002) 'Court culture and adjournments in criminal cases: a tale of four courts', *Criminal Law Review*, 1: 39–52.

Edwards, I. (2004) 'An ambiguous participant: the crime victim and criminal justice decision-making', *British Journal of Criminology*, 44(6): 967–92.

Fielding, N. (2006) *Courting Violence: Offences against the Person Cases in Court*, Oxford: Oxford University Press.

Freckelton, I. (2007) 'Death investigation, the coroner and therapeutic jurisprudence', *Journal of Law and Medicine*, 15(2): 242–53.

Jackson, J., Hough, M., Bradford, B. and Kuha, J. (2015) 'Empirical legitimacy as two connected psychological states', in G. Meško and J. Tankebe (eds) *Trust and Legitimacy in Criminal Justice: European Perspectives*, Cham: Springer International, pp 137–60.

Jacobson, J., Hunter, G. and Kirby, A. (2015) *Inside Crown Court: Personal Experiences and Questions of Legitimacy*, Bristol: Policy Press.

James, C. (2020) 'Towards a trauma-informed legal practice: a review', *Psychiatry, Psychology and Law*, 27(2), available from: www.tandfonline.com/doi/full/10.1080/13218719.2020.1719377

JUSTICE (2019) *Understanding Courts: A Report by JUSTICE*, London: JUSTICE.

Kaiser, K. and Holtfreter, K. (2016) 'An integrated theory of specialized court programs: using procedural justice and therapeutic jurisprudence to promote offender compliance and rehabilitation', *Criminal Justice and Behavior*, 43(1): 45–62.

Kirby, A. (2017) 'Effectively engaging victims, witnesses and defendants in the criminal courts: a question of "court culture"?', *Criminal Law Review*, 12: 949–68.

Kirby, A. (2019) 'Engaging with legitimacy: an examination of lay participation in the criminal courts', PhD thesis, University of Surrey, available from: http://epubs.surrey.ac.uk/851936/

The Law Society (2017) 'Access denied? LASPO four years on: a Law Society review', Law Society of England and Wales, available from: www.lawsociety.org.uk/support-services/research-trends/laspo-4-years-on/

McKeever, G. (2020) 'Comparing courts and tribunals through the lens of legal participation', *Civil Justice Quarterly*, 39(3): 217–36.

Ministry of Justice (2018) *Fit for the Future: Transforming the Court and Tribunal Estate*, London: MoJ.

Ministry of Justice (2019) *Response to 'Fit for the Future: Transforming the Court and Tribunal Estate' Consultation*, London: MoJ.

Mulcahy, L. (2013) 'Putting the defendant in their place: why do we still use the dock in criminal proceedings?', *British Journal of Criminology*, 53(6): 1139–56.

Mulcahy, L. and Rowden, E. (2019) *The Democratic Courthouse: A Modern History of Design, Due Process and Dignity*, London: Routledge.

National Audit Office (2014) *Implementing Reforms to Civil Legal Aid*, London: NAO.

National Audit Office (2018) *HM Courts and Tribunals Service: Early Progress in Transforming Courts and Tribunals*, London: NAO.

Owusu-Bempah, A. (2017) *Defendant Participation in the Criminal Process*, London: Routledge.

Owusu-Bempah, A. (2018) 'The interpretation and application of the right to effective participation', *International Journal of Evidence and Proof*, available from: https://doi.org/10.1177/1365712718780800

Rock, P. (1993) *The Social World of an English Crown Court*, Oxford: Oxford University Press.

Tyler, T.R. (2007) 'Procedural justice and the courts', *Court Review*, 44(1–2): 26–31.

Wexler, D.B. (2000) *Therapeutic Jurisprudence: An Overview*, 17(1): 125–34.

FOUR

Observed Realities of Participation

Jessica Jacobson

Introduction

The preceding chapters of this volume have discussed policy and practitioner perspectives on the legal principle that lay people should participate effectively in the judicial proceedings that concern them. This chapter is concerned with participation in practice, as observed by the research team across the range of courts and tribunals that are the focus of the study. After a short methodological note on the conduct of the observations, the chapter reports on differences between the variety of judicial settings, in terms of the institutional parameters of lay participation. This is followed by consideration of the commonalities across the settings. Here, it is argued that at the heart of almost every case observed by the researchers was a story of conflict, loss and disadvantage; and each lay court user's 'participation' in the case could be understood as a process by which they told, or had told on their behalf, their own version of that story. The final part of the chapter describes how judicial proceedings did not simply entail the *telling* of the court users' stories, but also their *translation* into legal questions and legal answers – and how this was a process which often had the effect of silencing and marginalising court users.

Observing court proceedings

The research team conducted a total of 316 hours' observation over the course of 90 visits to 17 venues covering the Crown Court, magistrates' courts, Family Court Employment Tribunal (ET) and First-tier Tribunal (Immigration and Asylum Chamber) (IAC). The venues were located across the three cities – one in Wales, two in England – and surrounding areas which had been selected as the main fieldwork sites (see Chapter One). During the visits, the researchers observed a total of 339 hearings in full or part, at which a total of 430 lay court users (witnesses or parties) were in attendance (see Box 4.1 for more details).

Box 4.1: Observations and court users

Crown Court

- 70 hours' observations over 20 visits to three centres;
- 69 hearings observed with 77 lay court users attending: 72 defendants (three unrepresented); five witnesses;
- characteristics of the 77 court users, as recorded by observers:*
  - 70 male; seven female;
  - 62 white; thirteen BAME; two ethnicity unknown;
  - 58 British nationality; six non-British nationality; 13 nationality unknown.

Magistrates' courts

- 97 hours' observations over 24 visits to three courts;
- 180 hearings observed with 187 lay court users attending: 184 defendants (24 unrepresented); three witnesses;
- characteristics of the 187 court users, as recorded by observers:*
  - 152 male; 32 female;

- o 147 white; 39 BAME; one ethnicity unknown;
- o 160 British nationality; 18 non-British nationality; nine nationality unknown.

Family Court

- 59 hours' observations over 18 visits to three hearing centres;
- 34 hearings (12 public law; 22 private law) observed with 64 lay court users attending: 59 parties (24 unrepresented); five witnesses/intervenors;
- characteristics of the 64 court users, as recorded by observers:[*]
  - o 29 male; 35 female;
  - o 52 white; 11 BAME; one ethnicity unknown;
  - o 52 British nationality; four non-British nationality; eight nationality unknown.

Employment Tribunal

- 49 hours' observations over 13 visits to four hearing centres;
- 17 hearings observed with 35 lay court users attending: 17 claimants (14 unrepresented); three respondents (one unrepresented); 15 witnesses;
- characteristics of the 35 court users, as recorded by observers:[*]
  - o 23 male; 12 female;
  - o 30 white; four BAME; one ethnicity unknown;
  - o 31 British nationality; four non-British nationality.

Immigration and Asylum Tribunal

- 41 hours' observations over 13 visits to four hearing centres;
- 39 hearings observed with 67 lay court users attending: 42 appellants (five unrepresented); four sponsors; 21 witnesses;
- characteristics of the 67 court users, as recorded by observers:[*]
  - o 34 male; 33 female;
  - o Nationalities: Afghani (eight), Indian (eight), Nigerian (six), British (five), Iraqi (four), Nepali (three), Rwandan (three), Bangladeshi (two), Chinese (two), Ghanaian (two), Ukrainian (two), US (two), Burundi (one), Dominican Republic (1), Iranian (1), Irish (1), Kenyan (1), Pakistani (1), Somali (1), Sri Lankan (1), Venezuelan (1), unknown (11).

---

[*] Gender, ethnicity and nationality were assessed on the basis of observed characteristics when they were not explicitly referred to in court.

In conducting the observations, the researchers usually sat in the public gallery of the court or tribunal room, or were sometimes directed by court staff to sit in sections designated for press or officials. Specific types of case or hearing were not targeted, but the researchers sought to attend a range of proceedings while concentrating as far as possible on those at which lay people were present and – where applicable – likely to give evidence. The researchers took detailed contemporaneous notes of proceedings (mostly by hand and subsequently typed up), guided by a template. The template prompted the recording of lay participants' backgrounds, characteristics, demeanour and interaction with the court during proceedings. Also recorded were substantive issues addressed in the hearing; the courtroom's physical lay-out and environment; the way practitioners presented and expressed themselves; presence or absence of legal representation, interpreters and supporters of the parties; and features of the case, such as adjustments for vulnerability.

The reported observations are necessarily subjective. They comprise a series of snapshots of proceedings, based on what was said in open court during the observations, and the researchers' interpretation of the behaviours of the (lay and professional) participants. Participants' views or background information on the cases were not collected (although occasionally practitioners provided unsolicited information[1]), and the researchers were very often unaware of the case outcomes. Nevertheless, the advantage of observation as a research method lies in the richness of the data which derive from an activity that 'goes beyond just seeing' to include also 'hearing and listening to, not just talk, but *soundscapes*', and maintains 'a sensitivity to physical environments and material things' (Atkinson, 2015: 40). Further, the researchers' use of a detailed template ensured that the observations were conducted as consistently and systematically as possible.[2]

As noted in Chapter One, this volume is being completed at a time of rapid expansion in the use of remote methods for court attendance, in response to the COVID-19 pandemic. The observational research provided only limited insight into the implications for participation of remote court attendance, since this was a feature of very few of the observed cases: just 15 of the defendants, and one witness, appeared by video-link in the observed criminal cases, while one party in the Family Court was meant to appear by video-link, but withdrew at the start of the hearing. However, brief consideration is given to this issue in the final section of the chapter, on 'Translation and disconnection'.

Institutional parameters of participation

It was immediately clear to the observers that the role of the lay court user in judicial proceedings varies greatly according to the jurisdiction to which the case belongs, the type of hearing within that jurisdiction and the court user's role or legal status. These intersect with a number of other factors setting the parameters of court users' participation, including:

- the kinds of parties (for example, individuals, corporate entities, the state) involved;
- the extent to which court users have elected to take part (such as ET claimants) or have no choice (as with defendants in criminal proceedings);
- the stake court users have in the outcome (which could be as significant as their liberty, access to their children or right to stay in the country; or could be minimal, as for witnesses with no sense of personal involvement in the case);
- whether parties are legally represented;
- rules of evidence;
- the degree of adversarialism of the process;[3]
- size, elaborateness and physical lay-out of venue in which the hearing is held.

The accounts in Box 4.2 illustrate the range of institutional factors which can shape a court user's participation. Each of these six hearings involved a lay party who had a different formal status and role: a bailed defendant on trial; a detained defendant pleading guilty and being sentenced; a parent in a contact dispute with his ex-partner; a parent in contested care proceedings; a migrant appealing against a refused asylum claim; and an ex-employee claiming unfair dismissal. Some of the cases additionally involved laypeople as witnesses, such as the two company employees who attended the ET hearing. The summaries also give some sense of the varied personal and social circumstances in relation to which the individuals found themselves caught up in judicial proceedings, and with which the court had to grapple in determining the outcome.

Box 4.2: Summaries of observed hearings

Case 1: Defendant giving evidence in sexual offence trial in Crown Court

Having been charged with sexually assaulting a much younger, female relative-by-marriage, the 58-year-old (bailed) defendant was appearing for trial in the Crown Court. The courtroom was ornate and imposing, with extensive wooden panelling, purple drapes, arched windows and a domed ceiling; it was one of many such courtrooms in a vast, Grade I-listed courthouse.

The defendant responded in a confident manner when taken through his evidence-in-chief by his defence counsel, and then during cross-examination when repeatedly pressed about his relationship with the complainant and the language he used (such as "Hello, Sexy") in exchanges with her on social media: "... None whatsoever ... I would *never* do that ... A complete fabrication ..." At the end of the day, with the trial due to continue the next, he left the courtroom with two family members who had been sitting in the public gallery.

Case 2: Defendant sentenced for theft in magistrates' court

The defendant was brought to the magistrates' court from police custody, charged with five counts of theft of clothing, food and some other items from various shops. He sat quietly in the glass-screened dock in the large, modern courtroom, as his defence solicitor agreed with the prosecution that, due to his severe drug habit, he had "an awful criminal record; I'd go so far as to say horrendous". The defendant spoke from the dock at the outset of proceedings to give his guilty plea, and at the end to confirm he understood his sentence (five short, concurrent custodial terms) and the arrangements for paying compensation. During a break in proceedings, he shared a joke with the two dock officers, at which all three laughed.

Case 3: Applicant father at interim hearing in the Family Court

A father had applied for contact with his 6-year-old daughter; she was living with his ex-partner, who did not attend the hearing. It took place in a small room that had the appearance of a personal office more than a courtroom, in which the District Judge (DJ) sat at a slightly raised, long desk, facing two advocates' benches. The room looked newly refurbished, in contrast to other parts of the court building: a civil justice centre situated in a side street, the shabby entrance to which could be easily overlooked from the outside.

The father, representing himself, spoke emotionally but eloquently about his daughter. At the end of the hearing, the DJ said that although she was currently unable to reach a decision – while another case involving the applicant and a different child and ex-partner was pending – she was pleased that the hearing had gone ahead as it had been "helpful ... to discuss it with everyone able to contribute". The father said "thank you", gathered up his papers into a plastic folder and left the courtroom.

Case 4: Respondent mother in contested care proceedings in the Family Court

In a large, modern courtroom, brightly lit through a floor-to-ceiling window taking up most of one wall, three long advocates' benches were populated by eight professionals: all women, all formally dressed. They included Cafcass (Children and Family Court Advisory and Support Service) officers, a local authority social worker and lawyers for all parties. The mother sat on her own on a fourth bench, until – some way into the hearing – the judge asked her to move forward.

A 'surveillance operative' was sworn in as a witness for the local authority and gave minutely detailed evidence about his and two colleagues' observations of the mother's movements on a day on which she had had permitted contact with her toddler son (currently in foster care). At issue was whether she had taken her son to visit her ex-partner who was believed to pose a risk to the boy. She later gave evidence herself and was cross-examined by the local authority lawyer who repeatedly accused her of lying. After the judge then ruled against her – stating the threshold was met for a care order – she continued to sit in silence for a few minutes, before abruptly getting up and leaving the courtroom without speaking to anyone.

Case 5: Appellant in asylum case in the IAC

An Iraqi Kurd who had been in the UK for the past ten years was appealing against a Home Office decision to refuse his protection claim. The hearing centre in which the case was heard was a characterless office block in a business park on the outskirts of a small provincial city.

In the small courtroom, the discussion between the Home Office Presenting Officer (HOPO), the appellant (through an interpreter), his lawyer and the judge covered various contested issues, including the appellant's lack of contact with family in Iraq; whether and how he might access identity documents from the Iraqi authorities; and his hand-to-mouth existence in the UK, dependent on the charity of a friend and the local Kurdish community. At the end of the hearing, after the judge said he was reserving his decision, the appellant anxiously pressed into his lawyer's hands a bundle of photocopied news reports on the deaths of people returned to Iraq, but both the lawyer and judge told him these were not relevant to the case.

Case 6: Claimant in unfair dismissal hearing in the ET

The unrepresented claimant was arguing that she had been unfairly dismissed by the large company for which she had worked for 26 years, latterly in a supervisory role. The hearing was held in a narrow, L-shaped courtroom on the second floor of a purpose-built, recently opened civil justice centre.

On day one of what was scheduled to be a two-day hearing, the claimant gave evidence and was cross-examined by the respondent company's barrister. The claimant then cross-examined two ex-colleagues appearing as witnesses for the company. Saying to the claimant that he "wanted to be fair because you are unrepresented", the judge offered explanations for technical terms that were being used; reworded as questions some comments she made to the witnesses ("I'm being [the claimant] for a minute," the judge said, before posing the questions); and checked with her that she had covered everything she needed to.

The diversity of modes and circumstances of participation reflected in the Box 4.2 summaries – which, across the full sample of observed cases, was multiplied many times over – does not render meaningless a generic concept of participation. Cross-cutting the jurisdictional and other divides, many commonalities to the hearings, and to the part played by laypeople within them, were noted. In line with the qualitative approach taken to the study as a whole, common features of the observed cases were not quantified. However, the snapshots of proceedings can be combined to create an overall picture of court user participation – to be presented over the remainder of this chapter.

Observed commonalities: stories of conflict, loss and disadvantage

Formal court and tribunal proceedings – including those in all the settings examined for this study – generally have as their immediate function the adjudication of disputes; albeit the performance of this function can be understood as of a much broader, 'symbolic' process whereby the 'rules' of wider society are stated, considered and refined (Steele, 1984: 202). The hearings observed by the researchers variously involved the adjudication of disputes between individuals, individuals and the state, or individuals and corporate entities. The *stage* of the adjudication process likewise varied widely – with many cases being at early, preparatory stages; others at a core decision-making stage; and others in a post-adjudication phase. But at issue in every case was a set of claims, and usually counter-claims, about harmful, unlawful, unfair or otherwise inappropriate behaviours or practices by one or more of the parties. Thus, what all hearings had in common was that they addressed situations in which the law had entered people's lives because 'the fabric of ordinary interactions [was] ruptured' (Ewick and Silbey, 1998: 77); or, to put it another way, they concerned circumstances and events gone wrong. It was also clear that the vast majority of cases involved individuals who were in need or disadvantaged in some way. Accordingly, almost every case had at its heart *a story of conflict, loss and disadvantage*; and each lay court user's 'participation' in the case could be understood as a process by which they told, or had told on their behalf, their own version of that story.

Conflict

In the court hearings observed for this study, the researchers saw the law being 'performed' so as to 'represent and replay social conflict and violence, turning history into dramatic narrative, fictionalizing social trauma, transforming it into the system of social representations, exchanges, surrogacies that make up the law' (Peters, 2008: 185). The final section of this chapter discusses the implications of this 'transformation' − or what is referred to here as 'translation' − of conflict, and associated violence and trauma, into legal questions and answers. But what is the nature of the conflict itself?

In the observed cases, the conflict underlying the claims and counter-claims being tested in court tended to be complex, multifaceted and entrenched. The ET's formal description of itself as 'an independent tribunal which makes decisions in legal disputes around employment law'[4] gives little sense of the scope of human drama and trauma that the disputes here frequently incorporate. One claimant, on day 11 of what was scheduled as a 15-day hearing of her claim of unfair dismissal as a school head, gave evidence about what she described as an 'agenda' among many of the school's governors and staff to force her out of her post. This, she said, followed disputes among staff, governors and the local authority about how the school was run, and child protection concerns she herself had raised. For their part, two witnesses appearing on behalf of the local authority described a long-running process involving disciplinary proceedings against the claimant, suspension and two appeals. Elsewhere, at a preliminary hearing, an ET judge argued that judicial mediation 'behind kind, closed doors' – a form of alternative dispute resolution – was the best option for addressing a claim of race discrimination. Both sides ultimately agreed to this, but not before the self-represented claimant, a Polish national, had insistently set out his case. When asked by the judge what he wanted, he said: "I want someone like you to listen to my story about what happened; I want them to apologise; I want justice." He described his former employment as a garage technician in which, he said, he had been subjected to racist comments (repeatedly dismissed as "banter"), accusations that his Polish qualification was fake and more general poor treatment – after several months of which he quit the job. The employer had thereafter instituted civil proceedings, claiming he had been overpaid and had taken annual leave without entitlement.

Many of the observed IAC hearings were appeals against Home Office decisions to refuse protection (or asylum) claims. In such cases, appellants' arguments typically centred on their experiences of actual or threatened extreme violence and persecution, often in the context of globalised conflicts and civil strife. For the observer, there was a marked incongruity between the usually muted ambience and anonymous setting of the tribunal and the discussion of places and unfolding humanitarian disasters that are otherwise familiar from international news reports. These hearings included that of a young Kurdish Iraqi man who, speaking through an interpreter, spoke of his father having been killed fighting for the Peshmerga (Kurdish militia), the demolition of his hometown by militant groups and threats he had personally received from ISIS. He had travelled to the UK, he said, in "a sealed vehicle, like a lorry, no windows; we couldn't see anything" and another vehicle "like a fridge-freezer lorry". The Home Office disputed his claim that his father had been a Peshmerga, and proposed his relocation to an area of Iraqi Kurdistan reported to be 'stable' and 'virtually violence free'. Another IAC appellant was a member of Afghanistan's marginalised Hazara community; he said he had been persecuted and imprisoned by the Afghan authorities following a legal dispute, and his brother had been killed. A woman from Rwanda told the IAC that her prior political activities would put her at risk if she was to return to the country. Through an interpreter, she said: "There's no peace in my country. My husband is in jail, one of my children is in jail … I don't have a job; they've taken my business; they've frozen my accounts." The Home Office argued, in response, that she was fleeing tax evasion charges, not persecution, in her home country.

The non-asylum hearings that were observed in the IAC did not address the kinds of extreme circumstances that were at the heart of asylum claims, but most nevertheless brought complex personal struggles and conflicts into view. Cases revolved around evidence put forward by appellants about family pressures and tensions, severe financial needs and health problems of many kinds. (As will be discussed later under the heading 'Loss and disadvantage', these were recurring themes across all the judicial settings visited.) At issue in several cases were Home Office allegations of sham marriages for immigration purposes, and of cheating (for example, through use of proxies) in the English language test required for visa extensions[5] – allegations strenuously denied by the appellants.

In the Family Court, the playing out of especially bitter and protracted conflicts was observed. In private law cases, these were typically disputes between estranged parents over contact or residence arrangements for their children. Allegations of serious domestic violence frequently formed part of these cases – demonstrating also the close interconnectedness between different parts of the justice system. Not only in family cases, but also in the course of ET and IAC hearings, references to criminal convictions or allegations were noted; and some of the observed defendants in the criminal courts were simultaneously embroiled in immigration or family proceedings.

Loss and disadvantage

The researchers found that the disputes adjudicated in courts and tribunals usually had their roots in, or at least had emerged in the context of, circumstances of loss and disadvantage. These circumstances encompassed very much more than the individual-level 'vulnerabilities' that are the main focus of special measures and other such provision for court users (discussed elsewhere in this volume). Among the wide array of court users' individual, socio-cultural and structural needs were those arising from: mental health problems; learning and behavioural difficulties; substance misuse; physical illness and disability; family and relationship breakdown; childhood trauma; bereavement; poverty; homelessness; prior offending or imprisonment; and prior experiences of discrimination, persecution and other forms of victimisation. For the most part, different forms of need and loss converged in individuals' lives, producing 'multiple layers of disadvantage' as have elsewhere been documented with regard to children in custody (Jacobson et al, 2010).

Multi-layered disadvantage was especially apparent with regard to the defendants appearing in many of the observed criminal cases. In case after case in the magistrates' courts, defendants charged with offences such as assault, theft and criminal damage were said to have profound, intersecting needs, including mental health and drug or alcohol problems, and chaotic and disorderly ways of living. In many cases of interpersonal offending, particularly violence, it was apparent that the contexts of the (alleged) offending encompassed victims and witnesses with comparable needs to those of the defendants.

Cases in which defendants were already in custody or another form of detention when charged with the offence provide a vivid illustration of the emergence of criminal proceedings from circumstances of loss and disadvantage. In these instances, the current case originated at a point at which the defendants had already lost their liberty. Among defendants observed in this situation was a woman being sentenced for assaulting a nurse in the psychiatric hospital where she was detained. In the same magistrates' court, a man pleaded not guilty over video-link from the prison where he was serving a prior sentence; he was charged with assaulting a prison officer whom he was said to have spat at. Elsewhere, another serving prisoner faced a charge of common assault on a prison officer – the offence having allegedly occurred when the officer entered his cell after he had failed a drugs test. He had originally been sentenced to imprisonment for public protection (IPP), and at the time of his court appearance had been in prison for more than ten years beyond the original 27-month minimum term he had received.[6] While at court, he initially refused to leave the cells in the basement of the building or to talk to his solicitor. In the courtroom, the district judge and defence advocate discussed the case: "He's a very difficult person as you've probably picked up this morning," the lawyer commented, adding: "I've failed to establish any rapport with this gentleman, which is unusual for me." The judge sympathised with the lawyer and observed that the defendant "knows he's playing the system … Game-playing: that's all it is."

In the course of care proceedings in the Family Court, as in criminal cases, concentrations of deep-seated needs and disadvantage in individual lives were laid bare. A circuit judge in one hearing centre dealt in quick succession with two such cases. In each case, the mother opposed the local authority's application for a care order with regard to a baby; in each case, also, many older siblings of the baby had already been removed from the mother's care. The local authorities had brought to the court's attention wide-ranging concerns about each mother's drug abuse and poor mental health, as well as domestic violence, emotional abuse and neglect of the children, and other problems (including a past allegation of sexual abuse) in the respective extended families.

Whether in criminal or family courts or in tribunals, the researchers found that court users' backgrounds of loss and disadvantage were usually integral to the substantive matter being considered in the proceedings: forming part of, for example, pleas in mitigation in the criminal courts that pointed to defendants' reduced culpability on grounds of mental ill health; arguments in the Family Court that parents lacked the ability to care properly for their children; claims of disability discrimination in the ET; and appeals against deportation to life-threatening situations in the IAC. Beyond this, the court process itself often had the effect of throwing court users' losses and disadvantages into ever sharper relief. It was apparent across the fieldwork settings that social, psychological, cognitive, emotional and other needs and vulnerabilities not only impeded court users' capacity to engage effectively with court proceedings, but were also heightened or exacerbated by the fact and nature of the individuals' involvement in those proceedings. (Discussion on 'Translation and disconnection', later, returns to this theme.) Thus, as has been previously suggested with regard specifically to the criminal courts, 'the courtroom is host not only to "vulnerable people", but also "vulnerable moments"' (Jacobson, 2018: 225).

If the disputes adjudicated in court had often arisen in *circumstances* of loss and disadvantage, it was also clear that the *outcomes* of the cases could consolidate or give rise to further disadvantage. Of course, the court and tribunal cases also offered the hope – and sometimes the reality – of redress for harms experienced and losses already incurred. For example, claimants in the ET could secure financial compensation or get their old jobs back; victims in the criminal courts could see offenders held to account for wrong-doing; and some parents in the Family Court stood to renew contact with or care for their children. Often, however, prospective losses were likely to outweigh any prospective gains.

For most of the court users (excluding those appearing as witnesses with little or no personal interest in the case), what was at stake in the proceedings was of great significance in their lives.[7] In the criminal courts, many defendants faced losing their liberty, should they be remanded or sentenced to custody. (Or, in the case of the defendant on an IPP sentence referred to earlier, a conviction would even further diminish the likelihood of release on parole at an undefined point in the future.) Defendants also faced other potential losses: restrictions on their freedom resulting from community penalties; financial loss if they were fined; and reputational damage. The last of these was of particular relevance in one hearing in which – in sharp contrast to the other observed court users – the defendant was exceptionally privileged: this was the high profile Crown Court trial of a celebrity charged with assault. In the Family Court, the stakes could be higher still: a life with or without one's children. A mother who was appealing against a previous decision by magistrates that she could have no direct contact with her two teenage sons – currently living with their father and his new wife – pleaded with the judge: "Give us a chance to be a family. Give me a chance to be with my children." But despite her claims as to the cruel behaviour of her ex-husband ("an imbecile" who had done "a hatchet job to get me and my family out of his life"), she lost the case: the judge determined that the existing (no contact) arrangements should continue, and passed an order preventing her from making further applications without permission from the court "because I am satisfied that both parties need a break from litigation".

In the IAC, it was their lives in the UK (and associated family ties and relative stability or safety) that appellants were striving to hold on to. This was a life which, one young woman from

India explained in appealing a Home Office decision to refuse her leave to remain, encompassed her marriage, house, recent birth of her baby and job for a clothing company. A Ukrainian husband and wife, who had been detained following their failure to comply with previous removal orders, applied for bail and appealed against the deportation. The wife became distressed and started crying when giving evidence and talking about the practical, domestic matters she needed to deal with – including arranging care for her cat, which had been left alone in their flat since their detention. Her husband responded scornfully when asked if he would appeal the removal decision when he was back in Ukraine, asserting that this would be like 'appealing to God when dead'. In an out-of-country appeal against refusal of leave to remain, by an elderly woman in Venezuela, the appellant's daughter acted as her 'sponsor' and gave evidence at the tribunal. She sobbed as she described her mother's deteriorating health following a series of strokes, and spoke of the inadequacies of the available health care in Venezuela. When asked how she would care for her mother in the UK, she replied: "Physical, emotional – I will look after her in every sense."

Telling the stories of conflict, loss and disadvantage

Thus far, this chapter has highlighted the commonalities across the cases observed in a wide range of judicial settings. It has been argued that these cases – whatever their diverse origins, nature and functions – concerned circumstances and events gone wrong; and that accordingly all cases had at their heart a story of conflict, loss and disadvantage. Most proceedings entailed the telling of competing versions of the story by the parties to the case and the assessment by the court or tribunal of which of the versions had the greater credibility or pertinence to the matters at hand. It was on this basis that the outcome of the case could be determined: whether this was a decision to continue or cease proceedings; to grant or dismiss a claim, appeal or application; to convict or acquit a defendant; or to pass one sentence or another on a convicted offender. The essence of a court user's participation can thus be understood to be the telling of their story – whether directly or through a representative – and the challenging of the other party's version of the story. This chapter now moves on to examine the scope of, and limits to, participation in this sense. The focus here is on the ways in which practitioners in the courtroom were observed to support and facilitate court users' participation.

Supporting and facilitating participation

Courts and tribunals operate in a highly pressured environment. It was evident during the observations that court lists were overloaded, paperwork was often missing and failures in technical equipment were common. Thus, it appears that the 'structured mayhem' observed some years before in research on the Crown Court (Jacobson et al, 2015) remains a feature of the courts and tribunals system. This is notwithstanding the endeavours by HMCTS, in the intervening period, to improve efficiency through the courts modernisation programme (discussed in Chapter Two of this volume). The findings of the observations and practitioner interviews (see Chapter Three) point to a range of factors relating to the reforms and accompanying austerity measures which undermine the effective operation of the courts – including court closures and the resultant increased workload of remaining courts and staff cutbacks. The increasing numbers of litigants-in-person (LiPs) in the courts, largely reflecting reduced availability of legal aid, pose their own challenges to the smooth and timely running of court business, on account of their particular needs for support and assistance during the court process.

Against this backdrop, the researchers repeatedly noted immense efforts made by practitioners in the courtroom – including judges, magistrates, lawyers, legal advisors and others – to help court users to participate in proceedings. As noted in Chapter Three, practitioners frequently spoke about the facilitation of court user participation as a significant part of their own and their peers' roles; and the observations of hearings provided ample evidence that this task of facilitation was indeed taken seriously and effectively carried out. This encompassed the assistance and support that practitioners proffered to the most obviously vulnerable or needy court users and to those who were LiPs; and, more generally, practitioners' humanising, sympathetic responses to the difficulties and pain revealed by the stories recounted in the courtroom.

A note of caution should, however, be added to this positive account of practitioner efforts to facilitate participation. It is possible that there was some degree of 'observer effect' which encouraged practitioners to treat court users with special care during the observed hearings. The visibility of the research team varied between settings and locations: in the criminal courts, there tended to be little interest in its presence, whereas court staff, the judiciary and sometimes lawyers were more aware of the researchers and the nature of their work in the tribunals and Family Court, where observers (unconnected to cases) are uncommon.[8] In one IAC hearing, the judge was so positively disposed towards the research that she asked the researchers, in a follow-up email, if they could provide "any feedback from the perspective of the appellant/witnesses".

Responsiveness to vulnerabilities and need

Use of formal 'special measures' or other adjustments to help vulnerable court users to give evidence was extremely rare in the observed family and criminal cases – and did not feature in any of the observed tribunal hearings.[9] In three of the observed family hearings, a screen was put in place to separate victims of domestic violence from the perpetrators.

In the criminal hearings, one defendant had an intermediary, while another was accompanied by a support worker who sat with her in the dock, and a vulnerable witness in one case appeared by video-link. In two Crown Court cases, a judge expressed scepticism about applications for an intermediary. In one of these, the judge said with some obvious reluctance that he would accept a CPS request for an intermediary for a 13-year-old complainant, adding that many such applications were unnecessary and undermining of advocates' skills in questioning vulnerable witnesses. He commented also that he found many intermediary reports to be "a cut and paste job".

Overall, however, it is likely that the observed limited recourse to formal adjustments in the criminal courts was largely a function of the type of hearings that the researchers attended – very predominantly plea hearings and sentencing proceedings, rather than trials – and did not reflect a general reluctance on the part of the courts to make use of the available provisions. Across the courts and tribunals, the researchers found that judges and others displayed awareness of court users' needs, a willingness to make ad hoc accommodations and a general sensitivity to what are referred to earlier as 'vulnerable moments', when court users displayed heightened distress, anxiety or anger.

This may be indicative of a generalised shift in judicial proceedings towards greater responsiveness to vulnerability.[10] The researchers noted, for example, encouragement of defendants, witnesses and parties to sit down and take breaks where they appeared to be under particular physical or mental strain; the dimming of lights in an ET hearing to help a claimant feel more at ease; a judge's calm reasoning with and securing of an apology from (rather than pursuit of a contempt of court charge against) a defendant who had lost his temper and told him to "go fuck yourself"; and the provision of careful explanations of the court process to witnesses who were evidently discomfited – including a 16-year-old boy with mental health problems who was giving evidence to the IAC in support of his parents' appeal. In a Crown Court trial, a defence barrister took the opportunity of a break in proceedings to tell the judge that his client had been having heart palpitations, at which the judge asked the defendant about his health and added: "giving evidence in the Crown Court, whatever the circumstances, is very stressful ... If you feel unwell, please say so." Also in the Crown Court, a 70-year-old woman pleaded guilty to charges of defrauding and stealing from a woman in her care. She sobbed loudly throughout, and received solicitous attention from both the court interpreter and a dock officer – the latter holding her by the arm to support her. After the judge passed a suspended custodial sentence, she continued to sob in obvious relief, while also – on leaving the courtroom – hugging and kissing two bemused-looking lawyers in attendance. In the IAC, judges were accommodating when appellants had young children with them – for example, permitting one woman to bring her baby into the courtroom.

Assisting litigants-in-person

As shown in Box 4.1, three out of the 72 defendants observed in the Crown Court were unrepresented, as were 24 of 184 defendants in magistrates' courts, 24 of 49 parties in the Family Court, five of 42 IAC appellants, and 14 of 17 claimants and one of three respondents in the ET.[11] LiPs were occasionally accompanied by representatives of voluntary organisations or personal acquaintances who provided support. Most obtained significant help in the courtroom from judges and legal advisors, sometimes including encouragement to obtain legal representation or, if that was not possible, advice from local pro bono or voluntary legal services.

Many judges took considerable care to explain procedures to LiPs. Some offered encouragement, like a Family Court judge who said to a father about the medical records he had supplied to the court: "You've assisted yourself greatly by doing that so promptly." They also offered reassurance ("Don't worry about that; we're taking it from square one," one ET judge told a claimant who had apologetically said he had never been in a court before) and practical guidance (another ET judge lent her own highlighters to a claimant, saying that the best way of preparing for his questioning of the respondent was to read through the latter's statement closely, and mark up those passages he disagreed with). Some judges, in an apparent effort to ensure equality of arms between represented and unrepresented parties, provided assistance that arguably amounted to a departure from the traditional judicial role of a neutral arbiter: like the ET judge quoted in Case 6 in Box 4.2, who reworded some of the claimant's questions and posed them to witnesses himself. The judge who lent the claimant her highlighters also, similarly, rephrased some of his questions: "This is the thing: you're not really asking questions – you're making statements. The question that *should* be asked there is: 'Do you remember him asking you ...?'"

A Crown Court case in which there was notable judicial intervention – in the form of strong encouragement to negotiate the basis for a guilty plea – concerned an unrepresented defendant charged with cultivation of cannabis in his home. Having heard the defendant's plea of not guilty, and inquired about the basis of his defence and his personal circumstances, the judge referred to the sentencing options and suggested the defendant discuss his plea with the prosecution advocate, who "will be fair". After a short adjournment, the defendant pleaded guilty and the judge sentenced him to a low-level community order, with some personal guidance ("It's not my role to give you lifestyle advice, but heed this. Cannabis is not good ...") into the bargain.

In a private law family case in which both mother and father were unrepresented, the legal advisor explained to them how the proceedings would run and said: "If you feel lost, do ask me." The father was serving a community order for violence against the mother, who had a restraining order against him; he was seeking to extend the limited contact he currently had with his sons. When it was time for him to question the Cafcass officer, the legal advisor stated some ground rules, including that he should allow her to finish answering one question before asking the next. Following this guidance, the father proceeded to challenge the evidence that had been presented by Cafcass in a careful and serious manner. In discussing the detail of contact arrangements, he said, "It works out now that I see them for about 3 hours per month after living with them for five years. This is very hard."

Humanising and sympathetic responses

Courteous and respectful treatment of court users was the norm across the range of court and tribunal settings, suggestive of a broad orientation (albeit this was likely to be implicit rather than explicit) of professional culture around the values of procedural justice.[12] Moreover, a great many practitioners dealt with court users in a manner that extended beyond courtesy and respect to kindness and sympathy, and an acknowledgment of the deeply personal and often highly emotive character of what was being addressed in the courtroom.

Humanising responses to court users' 'stories' were especially evident in the Family Court, where many of the rawest accounts of individual failings and interpersonal conflict were heard – as illustrated by the examples in Box 4.3 from public law cases. Perhaps with the aim of making proceedings feel less daunting and more congenial, parents in the Family Court were often referred to by judges and other practitioners as "Mum" and "Dad". This sometimes sounded incongruous in the context, and occasionally confusing – such as when one maternal grandmother was being questioned as a witness, and was asked with regard to her daughter: "How often do you see Mum?" "Did you see Mum in hospital?"

Box 4.3: Efforts to humanise care proceedings in the Family Court

Case 1

A mother was treated gently by lawyers, judge and Cafcass guardian[13] throughout a final hearing in care proceedings concerning her daughter. The mother, whose health problems included schizophrenia, cried when the judge asked her towards the end of the hearing if she had anything further to say, and she replied that she knew she was not a "100 per cent" good mother. The judge – who had earlier commented that the child was "delightful", which was a credit to the mother – told her in a kindly way that no mother is 100 per cent good.

Case 2

A social worker, while firmly making the case for a care order for a young child on the grounds of multiple, deep-seated problems in the home – referred to the "lovely baby ... Beautiful smile."

Case 3

In a complex case involving an application for an interim care order for a 14-year-old girl because her parents were unable to control her behaviour and she was putting herself at risk, the judge was at pains to express his sympathy for the father who was, the judge said, "as worried and upset as anybody I've seen in this court for a very long time".

Case 4

The judge congratulated a father on the "brave decision" he had made not to oppose a care order, and said warmly to two grandmothers who were involved in the case: "I don't know what we'd do without grandmothers like you."

Case 5

After a hearing which had dealt with an interim care order for newborn twins, there was a discussion among the parents, social workers and other lawyers in the lobby outside the courtroom. The lawyer for the Cafcass guardian asked the parents if she could see a photo of the babies: "I like to see what my clients look like." The father showed some pictures on his phone, and all the practitioners made appreciative comments: "Aww, so cute!"

Translation and disconnection

The findings set out in the previous section illustrate some of the ways in which practitioners help to ensure that court users' stories of conflict, loss and disadvantage are told in the courtroom. But of course, the telling of the stories is not the main goal of the judicial process – even if many practitioners assert, in line with procedural justice theory, that having a 'voice' is critical to a lay person's experience of justice (see Chapter Three). In the end, the court or tribunal must make a decision about the matters before it, and this must be a decision based in law; as legal philosopher Neil MacCormick states, 'Whatever question or problem is in our mind, if we pose it as a legal question or problem, we seek a solution or answer in terms of a proposition that seems sound as a matter of law, at least arguably sound, though preferably conclusive' (2005: 14). Posing a question or problem 'as a legal question or problem' necessarily entails a process of translation: during the legal proceedings, 'the real-life problem must be first translated, or transposed, into the language the law recognizes; only then – recognized by law – it may be solved, with these solutions resulting in real-life consequences' (Smejkalová, 2017: 65).

As the researchers observed court users' stories being translated into legal questions and legal answers, it became apparent that this process of translation was also a process which marginalised the individuals. Court language, concepts and structures had the combined effect of silencing court users, underlining the disparities between their social worlds and the social world of the courtroom, and ultimately disconnecting them from their own proceedings.

Complexity

Although some judges, lawyers and others sought to explain terminology and processes to court users (and especially LiPs), there was a notable tendency among many practitioners to default to jargon and complex language.[14] In the first case described in Box 4.3, where the judge was sympathetic and supportive towards an evidently vulnerable and distressed mother, this did not prevent references by lawyers to the "threshold document" being "not agreed, not opposed"; the child being "avoidant"; and the need to "progress contact in a dynamic way". In the second of the Box 4.3 cases, lawyers used traditional phrases such as "my learned friend" and (more than once, when turning away from the judicial bench to consult with their client), "I'll just turn my back." In this latter case, the maternal grandmother gave evidence; visibly shaking with nerves and tearful, she provided detailed responses to most questions, but occasionally struggled to understand: asking, for example, "What's 'abstinent'?" when being questioned about her daughter's drug use.

Formal and elaborate styles of language were generally more common in the Crown Court than in the other venues in which observations were conducted, exemplified by the following exchange between judge and defence counsel following the defendant's evidence-in-chief:

Defence counsel: "If I trespassed in that way, please forgive me."
Judge: "You have my forgiveness … You are forgiven, you are forgiven … [It was] an excess of enthusiasm."

Formality of language could combine with the complexity of issues or concepts under discussion to make it more difficult for lay parties to understand what was being said. Unusually, a Crown Court judge apologised to a defendant in a pre-trial hearing for the fact that much of what had been discussed would have been "quite incomprehensible", and explained that the defence and prosecution had had to make various arrangements in preparation for the trial. After sentencing an unrepresented defendant for two driving offences, a magistrate asked him if he had understood everything that had happened, to which the defendant replied, "All me head's fuzzy." The magistrate told him to see probation, who would explain everything.

Sentencing an offender with long-term addiction problems to a drug-related offence, a Crown Court judge spoke rapidly: "... totality ... cycle of addiction ... balancing aggravating and mitigating factors ... considerable licence period ..." The judge then asked the defendant if he had understood, who simply said "Yes." When another Crown Court judge passed sentence on a woman in her early 30s who had pleaded guilty to a serious assault, there was an extended discussion between the judge, probation officer and defence advocate about the defendant's accommodation, since both defendant and victim had been living in the same hostel. The judge eventually decided to make a restraining order (additional to the sentence) preventing the defendant from going within 100 yards of the hostel. It was agreed that she should present as homeless to the local authority and that her friend, who was at court, should collect her belongings from the hostel. When passing sentence, the judge spoke in a brisk but kindly way. He said that the defendant had "come to this court effectively a lady of good character" and the offence had been committed "out of your vulnerability and dependence on alcohol"; but it was clear she understood little of what was said. At the end, she twice asked from the dock: "Where will I stay? ... Can I go back to [the hostel]?" The judge could not hear the question; after it was relayed by the barrister, he reiterated that she was not to go within 100 yards of the hostel.

Silencing of court users

Most of the talking in the observed court hearings was done by the professionals in the room. Whether and to what extent lay court users communicated directly with the court or tribunal depended on a range of factors, including their role in proceedings, the type of hearing and case, and whether or not they were represented. Paradoxically, while participation is often assumed to depend on, or even to take the form of, being represented (see, for example, discussion of this in Chapter Three), it appeared that legal representation could also have the effect of undermining or even silencing the lay party's voice. While all court users were silent by the point at which the court made its adjudication, parties who were represented tended, by definition, to be silenced at an earlier stage in the court process than LiPs.[15]

In a private law case in the Family Court, magistrates considered a (represented) father's application for contact with his young daughter at the same time as the mother's application for a non-molestation order against the father. When the magistrate requested a Scott Schedule (setting out the issues under dispute), the mother's lawyer responded: "Ma'am, I think that's a sensible way forward – I can see the logic in your reasoning", and the father interrupted: "A what? Sorry – can I talk?" The magistrate said to him: "Well, you've got your representative." (Later, the magistrates decided to grant the mother's request for a non-molestation order, and went on to discuss dates for further consideration of the contact application; but the father put his head in hands, then leaned back in his chair, and said: "Just leave it. I'm not going to bother anymore.") A similar exchange took place in an IAC case – summarised as Case 5 in Box 4.2. After the judge stated that he was reserving his decision on the asylum appeal and the appellant would hear within two weeks, the appellant asked if he could speak, but was told by the judge to go through his lawyer. It was at this point that the appellant tried in vain to get both the judge and his lawyer to look at some news reports on the deaths of people returned to Iraq.

Represented parties could be silenced in other ways. In a different IAC hearing centre, another case involved a represented Iraqi appellant. Responding via an interpreter to questions from the HOPO, he spoke at length, with expressive tones and hand gestures. The HOPO complained to the judge that he was providing very long answers to short questions, leading the judge to say: "You are giving very long answers … I already have that information … only answer the questions you are asked." In a magistrates' court, the mounting distress of a defendant who felt her lawyer was not making her voice heard was evident. She was being sentenced for shoplifting various items from a supermarket, and had appeared at court from the prison at which she was already serving a sentence for assault. Crying in the dock during a break in proceedings, she repeatedly told her lawyer that she was getting help at her current prison for her drug problem and wanted to go back there so she could continue with the programme; the lawyer said there was little he could do about this, and she should relax and not worry. The defendant continued to cry and said the lawyer was not listening to her; he said the same of her. When the magistrate passed sentence shortly afterwards, nothing further was said about whether she would be returning to the same prison.

While LiPs were necessarily required to be more actively involved in proceedings than represented parties (and, as discussed earlier, were often given significant assistance), some nevertheless struggled to communicate. Particular difficulties could arise when both parties were unrepresented and each vied with the other to be heard. In one chaotic ET hearing, the complainant and respondent kept speaking over each other, with the former in particular finding it difficult to express himself; it also emerged that he had not brought the relevant documents to the tribunal. The atmosphere in one private law family case became very heated, with the two parents – both unrepresented – repeatedly interrupting and making accusations towards each other; until the judge lost patience and shouted at them: "Quiet! Stop interrupting! It's my turn!"

As noted at the outset of this chapter, there were too few observations of remote attendance to reach general conclusions about the implications for court users' engagement with proceedings. Of those cases involving remote attendance that were observed (in all but two of which defendants in prison or a police station were appearing in a criminal court by video-link), most proceeded without an obvious impact on participation, but some were problematic. The latter included a pre-trial hearing in the Crown Court, which provided an example of direct and literal silencing of a court user. The defendant, who was in prison, interrupted proceedings several times to assert that forensic evidence had been "planted" on him. Losing patience, the judge asked for the sound feed from the prison to be turned off. Similarly, the judge in another Crown Court pre-trial hearing threatened to turn off the sound as the defendant demanded over video-link: "Where's the TV, where's the jury? It's all a load of shit, innit ... I'm just stating the facts, d'you know what I mean?" After the threat was made, the defendant sat quietly for the rest of the hearing, just saying "OK, thank you," at the end. In another Crown Court, a defendant was sentenced over video-link to a 16-month custodial term for robbery. As the judge delivered the sentence – using a certain amount of jargon: "commensurate with the nature of the offence", "category range", "position aggravated" and so on – the defendant sat entirely silent and motionless, giving no indication of whether he understood what was being said.

Underlining the disparities

The references mentioned earlier are to generally courteous and respectful treatment of court users by practitioners. While this was the norm, the researchers also noted some interactions which underlined the social divide between the professionals and laypeople in court. The representative of an appellant in an IAC case chuckled when making his closing comments about his client's case, even while the appellant continued to cry openly about her children who – she had just told the tribunal – were living alone in Ghana. The researchers over-heard occasional disparaging or unsympathetic comments among practitioners after court users had left the courtroom; as when lawyers joked with each other about the unusual name of a baby who was the subject of care proceedings (during the hearing, the judge had asked the mother to confirm the spelling of the name and said, in a kindly way, "lovely name"). In the magistrates' court there was laughter at the end of a pre-trial hearing during which the defendant – a young woman charged with assaulting staff in her care home – had cried, shouted and sworn in the dock. Her lawyer said to the prosecutor and legal advisor: "I told you she was having a bad day!"

Not only were there apparent socio-economic, cultural and educational disparities between most court practitioners and most court users as individuals, but these disparities were embodied in court processes and procedures. It was clear that the language and styles of communication in court, along with the complexity, formality and ritualised nature of proceedings, and even court aesthetics (the grandeur of some courtrooms or court buildings, the formal dress of most practitioners), could all conspire to widen the gulf between the social world inhabited by court users and the social world of the courtroom.

The nature of this gulf between social worlds is illustrated by much of the observational data presented in the earlier discussions about court users' stories of conflict, loss and disadvantage, and the ways in which these stories played out in the courtroom. The observations gave rise to many further examples – among which some of the most telling were from the criminal courts. Here, many defendants immersed in cycles of disadvantage and offending behaviour often appeared to be largely impervious to the interventions (whether punitive or supportive) of the justice system.

A female defendant was observed pleading guilty to having breached her community order because of her failure to carry out unpaid work. A long-term heroin user, her ability to comply with the various requirements of the order was questioned by her defence solicitor, who referred to her chaotic lifestyle: she was living in a hostel, appeared to be continuing to use heroin – having dropped out of drug treatment, and had recently broken her foot. She had three children, of whom the eldest was about to be adopted. In the dock, the defendant admitted to having breached her order and gave a thumbs up to her partner – who was sitting, anxious and restless, in the public gallery – as the magistrates left the courtroom to confer. When the magistrates returned, the chair passed a sentence of 28 days' custody for her "wilful refusal to comply" with the community order. As she was escorted out of the dock, she shouted: "Do I do half?" Her partner replied: "You'll be out in 14," and the two blew kisses to each other. In another magistrates' court, there was discussion about the drug and alcohol use and mental health needs of a female defendant in her late teens said to pose "a high risk to known adults". Reference was made in court to a number of agencies which were involved in her care, and a mental health worker was in attendance at the hearing. The defendant was sentenced to 14 weeks' custody for an assault on her sister, having previously received a community order – with which she was not com-plying – for a similar offence against her parents. In the dock, she spent most of the hearing with her hood up and hand over her face. When passing sentence, the magistrate told her to stand up and look at him; she got to her feet, but closed her eyes. A male defendant in a plea hearing sat in the dock with his hands over his ears for much of the proceedings. As an interpreter tried in vain to communicate with him, the magistrates decided to remand him in custody pending his next appearance, scheduled for the Crown Court in several months' time. Cases like these raise the question of whether an active choice *not* to engage, or 'expressed rejection of the function of the courts' (Kirby, 2019: 167), might itself be considered a form of participation, and represent the exercise of agency by court users whose scope for action is highly constrained.

Several of the criminal cases observed – including the three just mentioned – made clear the inherent limitations of formal criminal justice responses to the multiple social, psychological and emotional problems with which much offending is associated. The *proportionality* of criminal justice responses to some of the offences observed coming before the courts could likewise be questioned. A defendant – said to have learning disabilities and to be "barely literate" – pleaded not guilty to a charge of breaching a restraining order because he had (possibly accidentally) sent his ex-partner a Skype contact request. The magistrates discussed arrangements for the forthcoming trial, and agreed to stand the case down in time for the defendant to make the coach for his 250-mile journey home. While questions as to the effectiveness and proportionality of judicial proceedings are outside the scope of the current study, the cases just cited point to the pertinence of the issue of court user participation to these much wider considerations.

Disconnection

In sum, it appeared that the process by which court users' stories were translated in the courtroom was also – by virtue of the complexities of court language and procedures, the silencing of court users, and the manifestations of the disparities between the court users' social worlds and that of the court – a process whereby individuals were gradually disconnected from proceedings and thereby marginalised. To deploy the theatrical analogy that is commonplace in discussion of the courts, court users can thus be said to move from centre stage to the periphery over the course of proceedings. This analogy is used by Smejkalová, who (as noted earlier) writes of real-life problems being translated 'into the language the law recognizes'. She describes 'the split role of the layperson' who is:

> at the same time a participant in a trial[16] where a specialized, subjectively incomprehensible language is used, while being an outsider, a spectator of this drama, not fully capable of accessing what is actually happening. She is physically on the stage but not fully participating

in the discourse; she has not fully entered the enclosed space, which is capable of producing the result to her dispute. (2017: 72)

A different perspective on the marginalisation of laypeople in court is offered by Owusu-Bempah (2020), who argues with reference to the criminal courts that the existence of 'barriers to meaningful communication between the defendant and the court' result in the situation where '[i]nstead of being viewed as the subject and key stakeholder of the criminal process, the defendant is often treated as an object on which the criminal law is imposed'. McKeever makes a similar point about appellants in tribunals. She notes that although various structural features of the tribunal system, particularly its 'relative informality', are intended to facilitate participation, in practice, 'legal decision makers adopt a legal perspective on what constitutes relevant information ... The result is that the appellant becomes an object in his/her own case rather than a participant in it' (2013: 579).

Conclusion

For scholars such as those just cited, the '*appearance* of participation' (McKeever, 2013: 578; emphasis added) may thus mask a reality of highly constrained engagement in judicial proceedings. In Chapter One of this volume, it is noted that effective participation in the court process is deemed, in law, to be essential to justice; and the previous chapter demonstrated that court-based practitioners are aware and supportive of this legal principle, even if they have varied understandings of the precise meaning and functions of 'participation'. What this chapter has shown is that, while many practitioners make considerable efforts to help court users participate in court, the forces militating against effective participation – arising from the very nature of the judicial process and the social and power differentials it exposes – are significant. The following, concluding chapter will consider what kinds of policy and practical reforms, at both national and international levels, could help to meet the attendant challenges to the fair and effective delivery of justice.

Notes

[1] Either in casual conversation or in the course of formal research interviews that coincided with observation visits.

[2] Other recent, UK-based studies involving structured observation of court hearings include Gill et al (2018) on asylum hearings; Trinder et al (2014) on litigants-in-person in private family law cases in England and Wales; McKeever et al (2018) on litigants-in-person in the civil and family justice system in Northern Ireland.

[3] While proceedings are generally adversarial, a semi-inquisitorial approach is sometimes followed; for example, for cases involving litigants-in-person (LIPs), the *Equal Treatment Bench Book* advises judges and magistrates to consider 'adopting to the extent necessary an inquisitorial role to enable the LIP fully to present their case' (Judicial College, 2020: 23).

[4] www.gov.uk/courts-tribunals/employment-tribunal

[5] Several of the observed IAC cases were in the aftermath of an investigation into organised fraud at English language test centres, which resulted in the revocation of tens of thousands of visas. A Public Accounts Committee report on the scandal found that 'the Home Office's flawed reaction to a systemic failure by a private company has had a detrimental impact on the lives of over 50,000 overseas students the Home Office accused of cheating' (Public Accounts Committee, 2019).

[6] The much-criticised IPP sentence was abolished in 2012, but the abolition was not retrospectively applied. As of 31 December 2019, 2,134 IPP prisoners remained in custody, of whom 93 per cent were post-tariff (Ministry of Justice, 2019).

[7] These are court users who, in Benesh and Howell's terms, have 'a very high personal stake in the outcome, but little control over it' (among whom they include 'criminal defendants, civil litigants, victims, and parties to domestic disputes'): a situation they found to be associated with low levels of confidence in (US) state and local courts (2001: 205).

[8] The tribunal hearings, like those in the criminal courts, were open to the public; however, tribunal staff – while welcoming – tended to be curious about our presence, tended to confirm with the judge that the observation could proceed. Approval was obtained from HMCTS and

[9] As discussed in Chapter Two, the Youth Justice and Criminal Evidence Act 1999 provided for a range of 'special measures' intended to assist vulnerable or intimidated witnesses to give evidence, including use of screens in the courtroom and live video-link, and intermediaries to facilitate communication.

thereafter the judge or magistrates in each individual case (who sometimes additionally sought consent from the parties) to conduct the Family Court observations.

[10] Which has been noted elsewhere with regard to criminal advocates (Hunter et al, 2018); see also Kirby (2017) and Henderson (2015).

[11] The disparities in proportions of LiPs between the different settings largely reflect the scope of legal aid provision. Publicly funded legal representation is available for most criminal defendants, parties in public law and some private law family cases, and appellants in asylum, but not (for the most part) immigration IAC cases. With very few exceptions, legal aid cannot be accessed for representation in ET cases.

[12] As discussed in Chapter Three, procedural justice theorists argue that legal authority is most likely to be regarded as legitimate by members of the public if they experience the *processes* of justice as fair – with fairness incorporating respectful treatment, having a voice and neutral decision making (Tyler, 2006, 2007).

[13] The guardian is appointed by Cafcass to represent the interests of the child in proceedings.

[14] The need for clearer communication in the courtroom, and the provision of information in simple, accessible language, is a particular focus of a recent JUSTICE Working Party report on improving participation by court users (JUSTICE, 2019).

[15] Owusu-Bempah has critiqued the general assumption, reflected in case law, that defendants' right to effective participation in their trial 'can be exercised by proxy through one's lawyer' (2018).

[16] She uses the term 'trial' to refer to 'any type of legal proceeding before a judge' (2017: 62).

References

Atkinson, P. (2015) *For Ethnography*, London: Sage.

Benesh, S.C. and Howell, S.E. (2001) 'Confidence in the courts: a comparison of users and non-users', *Behavioral Sciences and the Law*, 19(2): 199–214.

Ewick, P. and Silbey, S.S. (1998) *The Common Place of Law: Stories from Everyday Life*, Chicago: University of Chicago Press.

Gill, N., Rotter, R., Burridge, A. and Allsopp, J. (2018) 'The limits of procedural discretion: unequal treatment and vulnerability in Britain's asylum appeals', *Social and Legal Studies*, 27(1): 49–78.

Henderson, E. (2015) 'Communicative competence? Judges, advocates and intermediaries discuss communication issues in the cross-examination of vulnerable witnesses', Criminal Law Review, 9: 659–678.

Hunter, G., Jacobson, J. and Kirby, A. (2018) *Judicial Perceptions of the Quality of Criminal Advocacy*, London: Solicitors Regulation Authority and Bar Standards Board.

Jacobson, J. (2018) 'Balancing accessibility and authority: towards an integrated approach to vulnerability in the criminal courts', in P. Cooper and L. Hunting (eds) *Access to Justice for Vulnerable People*, London: Wildy & Sons, 219–233.

Jacobson, J., Bhardwa, B., Gyateng, T., Hunter, G. and Hough, M. (2010) *Punishing Disadvantage: A Profile of Children in Custody*, London: Prison Reform Trust.

Jacobson, J., Hunter, G. and Kirby, A. (2015) *Inside Crown Court: Personal Experiences and Questions of Legitimacy*, Bristol: Policy Press.

Judicial College (2020) *Equal Treatment Bench Book: February 2018 edition (March 2020 revision)*, London: Judicial College.

JUSTICE (2019) *Understanding Courts: A Report by JUSTICE*, London: JUSTICE.

Kirby, A. (2017) 'Effectively engaging victims, witnesses and defendants in the criminal courts: a question of "court culture"?' *Criminal Law Review*, 12: 949–68.

Kirby, A. (2019) 'Engaging with legitimacy: an examination of lay participation in the criminal courts', PhD thesis, University of Surrey, available from: http://epubs.surrey.ac.uk/851936/

MacCormick, N. (2005) *Rhetoric and the Rule of Law*, Oxford: Oxford University Press.

McKeever, G. (2013) 'A ladder of legal participation for tribunal users', *Public Law*, 7: 575–98.

McKeever, G., Royal-Dawson, L., Kirk, E. and McCord, J. (2018) *Litigants in Person in Northern Ireland: Barriers to Legal Participation*, Belfast: Ulster University.

Ministry of Justice (2019) *Offender Management Statistics Bulletin, England and Wales Quarterly: Prison Population: 31 December 2019*, London: MoJ.

Owusu-Bempah, A. (2018) 'The interpretation and application of the right to effective participation', *International Journal of Evidence and Proof*, 22(4): 321–31.

Owusu-Bempah, A. (2020) 'Understanding the barriers to defendant participation in criminal proceedings', webinar, 14 May, available from: www.law.ox.ac.uk/events/understanding-barriers-defendant-participation-criminal-proceedings

Peters, J.S. (2008) 'Legal performance good and bad', Law, Culture and the Humanities, 4: 179–200.

Public Accounts Committee (2019) *English Language Tests for Overseas Students*, London: House of Commons.

Smejkalová, T. (2017) 'Legal performance: translating into law and subjectivity in law', *Tilburg Law Review*, 22(1–2): 62–76.

Steele, E.H. (1984) 'Review: morality, legality, and dispute processing: Auerbach's "justice without law?"', *American Bar Foundation Research Journal*, 9(1): 189–205.

Trinder, L., Hunter, R., Hitchings, E., Miles, J., Moorhead, R., Smith, L., Sefton, M., Hinchly, V., Bader, K. and Pearce, J. (2014) *Litigants in Person in Private Family Law Cases*, London: Ministry of Justice.

Tyler, T.R. (2006) 'Psychological perspectives on legitimacy and legitimation', *Annual Review of Psychology*, 57: 375–400.

Tyler, T.R. (2007) 'Procedural Justice and the Courts', *Court Review*, 44: 26–31.

FIVE

Looking Ahead: Towards a Principled Approach to Supporting Participation

Penny Cooper

Introduction

This study began with a review of national policy, and in Chapter Two a picture emerges of fragmented policy development and procedural changes affecting court user participation. The focus of national policy development has been on criminal and family court users who are deemed 'vulnerable', although the definition has become increasingly fuzzy within the legal system of England and Wales and contrasts with usage of the term 'vulnerable' in other professional spheres. A major part of this study was made up of practitioner interviews and court observations through which four key research questions were addressed: in short, what does it mean for a lay person to participate in court, why does it matter, what promotes/inhibits their participation and what are the implications for participation of limited legal aid, court reform and the urgent shift to remote hearings in response to the COVID-19 pandemic?

Chapters Three and Four contain findings from 159 interviews and 316 hours of observations. This uncovered, for the first time, practitioners' concepts of court user participation. The result: *Ten Points of Participation* – six relating to form and four relating to function (see Chapter Three, Box 3.1: Conceptualisations of Participation and at Table 5.2: Ten Points of Participation as a provisional framework for court user guidance). Observational data provided many examples of practitioners' sympathetic and respectful treatment of court users, as well as their efforts to promote and support court user participation. Notwithstanding, there remain significant barriers to participation – for example, lack of legal representation, complex law and procedure, and impenetrable legal language in the courtroom.

This chapter addresses the fifth and final research question: What future developments in policy and practice, across the justice system of England and Wales and beyond, could ensure that participation is better supported? In order to take a broad perspective when addressing this question, an international review of initiatives for young or otherwise vulnerable witnesses was conducted. The aim was to explore what England and Wales might learn about supporting participation from other jurisdictions, as well what other jurisdictions might have learnt from England and Wales. The review revealed multiple examples of international 'export' of practices, including canine support for witnesses in court, witness intermediaries and ground rules hearings, as well as learning opportunities from remote witness assessments being conducted in New South Wales, Australia. This chapter also considers adaptations to hearings as a result of the initial COVID-19-related emergency changes to court proceedings. In conclusion, it is argued that, while it has been easy to pay 'lip service' to *effective participation* in law and practice, it is harder to gain an understanding of what it means in practice. New principles are recommended for future research and policy development so that court user participation may be central to future court reform.

International review

The international review aspect of this study incorporated a literature review (the methodology for which is detailed later), as well as information gathered on international trips.[1]

Methodology for the literature search

The Westlaw UK database was searched[2] for innovative measures/adjustments for court users. It was apparent that 'vulnerable' is not a universal term used to refer to witnesses for whom adjustments are made; therefore, the search included, but was not limited to, references to 'vulnerable' witnesses or parties.

In order to focus on recent developments and a manageable volume of results, only publications after 1 January 2016 in the English language were included in the Westlaw sweep. The Westlaw search resulted in a return of 308 journal articles. After an initial perusal of the titles of the articles and their abstracts, a total of 11 recent articles were identified as relevant. The Google Scholar research resulted in 113 publications. Article abstracts were reviewed for relevance and, once duplicates as compared to the Westlaw UK results were excluded, two further articles were identified as relevant. In addition to the Westlaw UK search, numerous permutations of the search terms were entered into Google Scholar, Google and Twitter in a quest for other published material, including news stories, reports, educational videos and guidance.

The international review identified six types of initiative aimed at promoting participation of vulnerable court users:

- witness intermediaries;
- ground rules hearings;
- therapy and court facility dogs;
- pre-recording witness testimony in full;
- specialist hearing suites;
- specialist guidance for judges.

All six initiatives seek to alter for the better the interaction or the circumstances of the interaction between the court user and the practitioners in a hearing.

Witness intermediaries

The term 'witness intermediary' is used in this section to describe someone who helps convey questions to and answers from a witness. However, the intermediary role described here takes a variety of forms: some intermediaries relay questions, others conduct the questioning themselves, others help plan communications and only step in if questioning breaks down. All the roles aim to reduce anxiety and/or promote good quality communication. In England and Wales, eligibility is related solely to age or incapacity, but elsewhere (as for example in New South Wales, Australia) it may also be restricted to witnesses in particular geographical locations and types of cases.

In South Africa, the role was established for child witnesses in 1992, with the aim of reducing the trauma associated with giving evidence. There, the intermediary accompanies the child witness in the video-link room, translating and relaying questions into child-appropriate language, 'buffering aggression and intimidation and informing the court when the witness tires or loses concentration in order for the presiding officer to adjourn the court' (Jonker and Swanzen, 2007: 95).

In Norway, the intermediary is a specialist forensic interviewer who is observed by the judge and counsel from an adjoining room via video-link or one-way glass. After their interview, the intermediary consults with the judge and counsel, who are given the opportunity to suggest topics to be covered or contradictions to be explored. The interviewing intermediary returns to question the child on the agreed topics until all are satisfied (Hanna et al, 2010: 10). In Sweden, evidence can be taken from children in advance of the trial in a procedure controlled by an examining magistrate. Israel also has a system of child examiners or 'youth interrogators' who collect evidence from children for use in court (Spencer and Flin, 1990).

In 2019, Chile implemented new legislation aimed at enabling child witnesses to give their best evidence, which includes a provision for witness intermediaries. This development sits against the backdrop of Chile's transition from an inquisitorial to an adversarial legal system as it has sought to incorporate 'respect of human rights and international standards' (Gómez, 2010). Law 21.057 regulates the treatment of children and adolescents[3] who are complainants in sexual abuse cases. Article 3 of 21.057 sets out the *six principles* of application which can be summarised as follows:

- creating conditions at trial that are in keeping with the child/adolescent witness's best interests;
- supporting their right to be heard;
- supporting their voluntary participation as a witness;
- preventing their secondary victimisation by creating an environment which is appropriate to their individual needs;
- the timely investigation and prioritisation of a case involving a child's/adolescent's complaint;
- safeguarding the dignity of every child/adolescent.

The parties, their lawyers and the presiding judges remain in a traditional courtroom linked by closed-circuit television to the witness. The lawyer states a question, the judge repeats it in a form that they are content with and the intermediary hears the question (as conveyed by the judge) through an earpiece and repeats it to the witness. The witness will neither see nor hear what is happening in the courtroom. However, the court can see and hear the intermediary via the TV link.

Chile's intermediary model is similar to South Africa's; the question is relayed by a neutral person using a calm pace and tone. However, Jonker and Swanzen reported that in South Africa the use of an intermediary relaying questions has shortcomings, which have given rise to a number of problems:

The power of the intermediary is very limited, since the intermediary is perceived to be nothing more than an interpreter (and not an expert witness) and the court can at any time insist that the intermediary repeat the question exactly as it was phrased. A further disadvantage of the present system is that the intermediary does not have the authority to comment on a question and give an opinion as to whether a child understands a question or not. The intermediary is powerless to intervene and argue that questions should not be asked in a particular sequence or not phrased in a certain manner. (2007: 106)

At the time of writing, the Chilean intermediary model has been operational for under a year and a protocol allowing the intermediary to intervene is being trialled.

Witness intermediaries have been available in England and Wales since 2003 (see Chapter Two). Their role, as set out in section 29 of the Youth Justice and Criminal Evidence Act 1999, is to communicate the questions to the witness and the replies given. This version of the intermediary role, 'the English model', consists of the intermediary assessing the communication needs and abilities of the witness and advising practitioners how best to accommodate those needs and abilities. In contrast to the role in the jurisdictions described earlier, the intermediary in England and Wales does not undertake forensic questioning, although they closely advise and support those who do. Research has demonstrated how intermediaries in England and Wales enable a witness to provide and questioners to elicit more accurate and complete information (for example, Wilcock et al, 2018). In court hearings, intermediaries make recommendations for ground rules for questioners to follow and intervene only if communication breaks down. (The international evolution of the ground rules hearing is discussed later.)

The English intermediary model has been successfully adopted in modified form in Northern Ireland and in the states of New South Wales, Victoria (Cooper and Mattison, 2017) and the Australian Capital Territory. Since 2016, in the Australian state of New South Wales, reflecting the geographic dispersal of witnesses and intermediaries, many witness assessments are conducted remotely using video technology. Plans for an intermediary scheme in Tasmania are at an advanced stage, while South Australia is moving from a volunteer communication partner scheme to a 'fee-for-service' model (Parliament South Australia, 2020). New Zealand has also implemented its own version of the English intermediary model, and research has found that professionals are overwhelmingly in support of the new role (Howard et al, 2019).

Professionals in India are said to be exploring the use of the English model of the intermediary (Shukla, 2018), although the applicable guidelines for a vulnerable witness communication facilitator are more akin to the South African model where the intermediary relays the questions:

> the respective counsels for the parties shall pose questions to the vulnerable witness only through the facilitator, either in the words used by counsel or, if the vulnerable witness is not likely to understand the same, in words or by such mode as is comprehensible to the vulnerable witness and which convey the meaning intended by counsel. (Delhi High Court, nd: 9–10)

The Republic of Ireland has legislation which allows for the use of an intermediary, but it is 'seldom used' (O'Leary and Feely, 2018). In at least one criminal trial in the Republic of Ireland in 2016, the services of an English intermediary were used (Gallagher, 2016). Intermediaries operating under the 'English model' have also assisted on an ad-hoc basis in cases in Jersey (Channel Islands), Scotland and British Overseas Territories.[4]

While the use of witness intermediaries appears to be growing in popularity, there is relatively little published research on their effectiveness and no known research comparing the effectiveness of the different models described earlier.

Ground rules hearings

> The English approach of a ground rules hearing prior to the recording session, at which lines of questioning are agreed seems to have merit; for this to work well, the bench must be prepared to take an active role in setting the parameters for the cross-examination and re-examination of the witness. (Scottish Court Service, 2015: 36)

Ground rules hearings (also discussed in Chapter Two) are a judicial case management tool for setting the parameters for the treatment of a witness or party at a hearing so that they may participate effectively. The practice originated in England and Wales when a ground rules meeting/hearing was requested by witness intermediaries (Cooper et al, 2015). Ground rules hearings and subsequent planning of questions in line with the ground rules should be a collaborative exercise.

> The ground rules hearing should cover, amongst other matters, the general care of the witness, if, when and where the witness is to be shown their video interview, when, where and how the parties (and the judge if identified) intend to introduce themselves to the witness, the length of questioning and frequency of breaks and the nature of the questions to be asked. (*R* v *Lubemba*; *R* v *JP* [2014] EWCA Crim 2064, para 43)

Ground rules hearings, an established feature of the English legal system in cases where court users are deemed vulnerable, feature in the criminal justice systems in Scotland and three Australian states. They have been incorporated into primary

Table 5.1: Comparing approaches to ground rules hearings

Jurisdiction	Ground rules hearing procedure statute, rule or practice guidance	Year procedure was first written into statute, rule or practice guidance
Criminal Justice System, England and Wales	Criminal Procedure Rules, Rule 3.9(7) (see also Criminal Practice Direction, paragraph 3E).	2014
Family Justice System, England and Wales	Practice Direction 3AA Vulnerable Persons: Participation in Proceedings and Giving Evidence, paragraphs 5.2–5.7.	2017
Criminal Justice System, Victoria, Australia	Criminal Procedure Act 2009, Part 8.2A – Ground rules hearings and intermediaries, page 23, paragraph 13.	2018
Criminal Justice System, News South Wales, Australia	Criminal Trial Courts Bench Book, District Court Criminal Practice Note 11.	2019
Criminal Justice System, Australian Capital Territory	Evidence (Miscellaneous Provisions) Amendment Act 2019, Part 2.	2019
Criminal Justice System, Scotland	Vulnerable Witnesses (Criminal Evidence) (Scotland) Act 2019, section 1ZD.	2019

legislation in Scotland and two Australian states (Victoria and the Australian Capital Territory). Legal provisions for ground rules hearings differ according to the jurisdiction, although all have their origins in the ground rules hearing concept created[5] in England and Wales (Table 5.1).

In a unique piece of legislative drafting, the Australian Capital Territory ground rules hearing provision is applicable to all witnesses in criminal proceedings:

A court may, at any time, if satisfied that it is in the interests of justice, direct that a ground rules hearing be held for a witness in a criminal proceeding.

...

(1) At a ground rules hearing for a witness in a criminal proceeding, the court may make any direction the court considers is in the interests of justice, including any of the following:

(a) a direction about how a witness may be questioned;

(b) a direction about how long a witness may be questioned;

(c) a direction about the questions that may or may not be asked of a witness;

(d) if there is more than 1 accused – a direction about the allocation among the accused of the topics about which a witness may be asked;

(e) a direction about the use of models, plans, body maps or other aids to help communicate a question or an answer;

(f) a direction about the use of a support animal by the witness;

(g) a direction that if a party intends to give evidence that contradicts or challenges the evidence of a witness or that otherwise discredits a witness, the party is not obliged to put that evidence in its entirety to the witness in cross-examination. (Chapter 1A Ground rules hearings – criminal proceedings 4AB(1) and 4AF)

Support animals (see (f)) are available to help calm anxious witnesses when they give evidence, but are also available to witnesses waiting outside Canberra criminal courtrooms.

International approaches to the provision of canine support both inside and outside the courtroom are discussed in the following section.

Court 'facility dogs'

It is important to note the difference between 'therapy dogs' (also known as 'companion dogs') and 'facility dogs' in the justice system. Therapy dogs support a witness before and/or after an investigative interview or hearing. Facility dogs accompany a witness while the witness gives evidence and are specially trained to do so. The two are closely connected, but it is the facility dog which can have a direct effect on participation in court.

> [Facility] dogs are specially trained to a high standard and are allowed in actual police interviews or courtrooms ... [Therapy] dogs should not go beyond providing comfort in waiting rooms before or after an interview/trial. Due to their lack of training and unpredictability, they are not suitable to be present during a police interview or during court proceedings. (Spruin and Mozava, 2017: 39)

The first recorded instance of a *facility* dog being used to support a witness in court was in the US state of Mississippi in the early 1990s (Spruin, 2016). Their use has spread to most other US states; however, evidence supporting the use of facility dogs remains sparse. Grimm argues that the use of facility dogs for child victims is 'constitutionally suspect' and should be excluded on account of the availability of other support mechanisms, such as videotaping of testimony, video-link, dolls, stuffed animals and child advocates (2013: 292). Conversely, it has been argued that facility dogs 'fill a gap for witnesses when traditional comfort items and support persons fail to ease their anxiety' (Holder, 2013: 1187). Six attorneys interviewed for a small US study supported the provision of witness support by court dogs, although one respondent noted that they should also be available for the defence, not just prosecution witnesses (Donaldson, 2017). A study with mock jurors provides initial evidence to suggest that facility dogs 'may not prejudice jurors against defendants or bias jurors in favour of the witness they accompany' (Burd and Mcquiston, 2019: 11).

A survey of US and Canadian criminal justice system practitioners who had experience interviewing child witnesses with and without the use of a facility dog found that 'respondents believed that utilising facility dogs both enhanced witnesses' credibility and helped [forensic] interviewers to build rapport with witnesses' (Spruin et al, under review).

The presence of a facility dog providing the witness with support in court has been recognised in at least three US states (National Crime Victim Law Institute, 2013). In 2013, in *State of Washington, Respondent* v *Timothy Dye, Petitioner No 87929–0,*[6] the Supreme Court of Washington said:

> Generally, we give trial courts wide discretion to control trial proceedings, including the manner in which testimony will be presented. We recognize that some trial procedures, such as providing a child witness with a toy on the stand or shackling a defendant at trial, may risk coloring the perceptions of the jury. But trial courts are capable of addressing these risks. Here, the trial court acted within its broad discretion when it determined that Ellie, the facility dog provided by the prosecutor's office to the victim Douglas Lare, was needed in light of Lare's severe developmental disabilities in order for Lare to testify adequately. (Para 1)

The Courthouse Facility Dogs Foundation in the US cites 234 facility dogs working in 40 of the 50 states as of 27 November 2019 (Courthouse Dogs Foundation, 2020), a substantial increase on their previously published figure of 148 dogs in 35 states as of 19 September 2017.

In Chile, a facility dogs program has been running since 2009, having started in conjunction with the Courthouse Dogs Foundation which provides professional training to the Chilean Bocalan Trust.[7] The Courthouse Dogs Foundation also reports (2020) that the Australian state of Victoria's Office of Public Prosecutions has a facility dog. Best practice recommendations for wider implementation in Australia have been made (Morrison, 2019). Dogs also support witnesses in court in Canada (Grant, 2014; Warnica, 2015) in eight out of 13 provinces (Courthouse Dogs Foundation, 2020). In *R v Marchand and Marchand*,[8] a 14-year-old complainant in a sex offence case was accompanied by a dog alongside the dog handler in the witness box:

> The testimony of the handler included evidence of the effectiveness of service dogs such as Caber in situations similar to the one before the court. The evidence was compelling that service dogs such as Caber have a calming influence on witnesses who must testify about difficult matters, and that these dogs allow the witness to effectively communicate his or her evidence, without creating interference or distraction. (Para 5)

In one small Canadian study, seven court officials perceived the use of a courthouse facility dog to be beneficial for children and young people who are experiencing challenges testifying in court; the study also called for further evidence-based research on the use of dogs in court to support vulnerable witnesses (Glazer, 2018: 52).

Although not part of a formal scheme providing facility dogs, a young witness's autism support dog accompanied them in the video-link room in Northern Ireland in 2018. The dog sat behind the witness's chair while they gave evidence.[9] The intermediary, who had made the recommendation for the dog to be present, reported that the witness coped very well and did not need to stroke the dog. This is the first known instance of a dog in the video-link room in the United Kingdom. It is also known that a dog accompanied a vulnerable witness to give pre-recorded evidence in a criminal matter in Sydney, Australia.[10] These two examples did not involve a dog specially trained for the courtroom; rather, they were instances of ad-hoc applications for canine support which the judge granted. Belgium, France and Italy also have facility dog schemes (Courthouse Dogs Foundation, 2020) and in England, for research purposes, Dr Liz Spruin has 'imported' a specially trained facility dog from the US.[11] These are small steps towards more expansive use of facility dogs to support witnesses in hearings.

Pre-recording witness testimony in full

Pre-recording of witness testimony may be partial or full. Full pre-recording includes not only the witness giving their account (commonly referred to as evidence-in-chief), but also the witness's responses to an opposing party's challenge to that account (commonly referred to as cross-examination). Of all the special measures for vulnerable and intimidated witnesses in criminal courts in England and Wales, this was the last to be introduced. While the pre-recording of interviews in place of evidence-in-chief is a long-standing practice for eligible witnesses, pre-recording of cross-examination only began in 2014 in pilot courts (see Chapter Two). By 2018, technological difficulties were delaying roll-out in England and Wales (Cooper and Mattison, 2018). Contrast Australia, where, although each state has its own particular eligibility criteria and procedures, pre-recording of child witness evidence in its entirety is commonplace in criminal cases and has been for years in most states (Corish, 2015: 187).

Reviewing the practice of pre-recording the testimony of child witnesses in criminal cases in Australia, Norway and England and Wales, the Scottish Court Service's 'Evidence and procedure review' noted that practitioners are 'convinced that there are clear benefits to be had from a systematic and structured approach to the use of audio-visually recorded forensic interviews as a witness' principal evidence, and from the recording of cross-examination' (2015: 25). The review's vision for recording child witness evidence in its entirety was realised in the Vulnerable Witnesses (Criminal Evidence) (Scotland) Act 2019. This requires the court to enable a child's evidence to be given (and recorded) in advance of the hearing in front of a specialist judge unless it is an exceptional case.

Specialist hearing suites

Some courts have a specialist approach to particular kinds of cases; for example, Family Drug and Alcohol Courts (England and Wales) take a therapeutic, problem-solving approach to cases, which means the focus is not only on finding the best care plan for the child, but also on substance misuse treatment for the parent. Other courts taking specialist approaches are operated by practitioners specifically trained to deal with certain cases – for example, sexual offences courts in India and in Antigua and Barbuda. The international review also revealed examples of innovative, specially designed, calming environments aimed at supporting court user participation where the complainant is a child.

The Goa Children's Court, which has been operating for some 16 years, has pink walks and the judge's table is placed so that the child can 'sit near the judge rather than across from her'. Delhi has gone even further; children can 'wait in a separate room designed like a crèche with toys and colouring material; the courtrooms have one-sided glass booths so the accused can see the proceedings, as is their right, but the child does not have to see the accused' (Sriram, 2017). There are parallels with the new Glasgow Evidence and Hearings Suite. Opened in November 2019, it was designed to enable child witnesses to pre-record their evidence and for vulnerable witnesses to give evidence remotely away from the formality of a traditional courtroom. The suite includes a calming 'sensory room' with special furnishings which can be also be used as a remote video–link room. There is also an evidence room with one–way glass so that a child witness can be observed being questioned. Similar suites are planned elsewhere in Scotland (SCTS, 2019; BBC, 2020a).

Specialist judicial guidance

There are diverse examples from overseas of publicly available judicial guidance aimed at supporting participation. Guidance may be relatively brief and broad in scope; for example, Colorado's 'Access to the courts: a resource guide to providing reasonable accommodations for people with disabilities for judicial officers, probation and court staff':

> This directive is issued to ensure equal access to and full participation in court and probation services and programs by people with disabilities, including attorneys, litigants, defendants, probationers, witnesses, victims, potential jurors, prospective employees and public observers of court proceedings. (Colorado Judicial Department, 2004: 4).

The 15-page resource highlights a wide range of adaptations, including talking slowly, writing things down, taking periodic breaks, 'scheduling court proceedings at a different time to meet the medical needs of the individual; providing a coach or support person at the proceeding; or allowing videotaped testimony or the use of video conferencing technology in lieu of a personal appearance' (Colorado Judicial Department, 2004: 9).

California Courts' 'Elder abuse pocket reference guide' (Mosqueda and Judicial Council of California, 2012) focuses on the needs of a specific cohort of court users and runs to 106 pages. It contains not only legal but also medical guidance for those dealing with elder abuse cases.

The Judicial Education Institute of Trinidad and Tobago publishes particularly extensive guidance, including a 311-page *Criminal Bench Book* on the JEITT E-book platform (2015) and a 113-page 'Gender equality protocol for judicial officers' (2018). A section titled 'Use of alternative means of giving evidence' states that for complainants in cases of sexual offences and for children:

> video conferencing, video digital recording, depositions taken by the Registrar or a Master using computer-aided transcription or audio-digital recording or both, telephone or other alternate electronic means including telecommunications application software using Voice Over IP. (Judicial Education Institute of Trinidad and Tobago, 2018: 78)

The status of the guidance is described within the document:

> It simply represents suggestions on the best practices to be adopted when faced with inequality as a result of gender or any other source of discrimination. It seeks to provide the Judicial Officer with guidance on how to approach adjudication in a manner that will allow for more than just a strict application of the laws. (2018: IV)

In India, 'Guidelines for recording of evidence of vulnerable witnesses in criminal matters' (nd) is a 19-page document emanating from the High Court: 'The purpose of this protocol is to present guidelines and mandatory recommendations, to improve the response of the justice dispensation system to vulnerable witnesses' (Delhi High Court, nd: 2). The protocol provides an overview of potential adjustments: a person appointed by the court to attend to support the witness, prohibition on the publication of the child witness's identity, comfort items, courthouse familiarisation tour, meeting the judge, communication ('descriptive aids'), video-link, screens, image or voice altering or any other technical device.

Reflections on innovative support for participation

The cross-fertilisation of ideas from one jurisdiction to another, though widespread, has also tended to be ad hoc and unco-ordinated. International initiatives described earlier, as well as national policy developments described in Chapter Two, share common features. They are as follows:

- Slow to spread: initiatives have frequently taken years, sometimes decades, to be more widely adopted in new jurisdictions.
- Under-researched: their effectiveness is rarely the subject of academic study.
- Niche: they have been applied only to court users deemed vulnerable enough to need special assistance.
- Temporary 'fixes': the traditional mores of court culture which dictate how most court users participate remain unchanged.

While there is a multitude of national and international developments which have a clear goal of enhancing partici-pation, few are explicitly grounded in a theory/principles of participation. Practitioners' contrasting accounts of what par-ticipation entails and why it matters, set out in Chapter Three of this volume (see, in particular, Box 3.1), provide a provisional framework – elaborated later as the *Ten Points of Participation*. This framework requires further elaboration through research with court users which could, for example, examine the extent and impact of enduring barriers to participation such as the language, formality and emotional stakes in the courtroom. It is hoped that framing participation according to these ten points will take us on a route to a better understanding of *effective participation*, but there is still some way to go.

National policy developments for vulnerable witnesses were originally justified not because they would enhance participation, but for more practitioner-centric reasons – because it was thought they would improve the quality of a witness's evidence. In the 20 years since special measures were first introduced, the legal narrative on adaptations in court has begun to focus more on *effective participation*, but without concomitant attention to what it means to participate and to do so effectively. This study has explored practitioners' conceptions of participation. What participation means to court users and what makes it *effective* is much talked about, but remains too little explored. Taking an idea from the world of gardening,[12] the best time to address effective participation of court users was 20 years ago, and the second best time to address it is now.

In England and Wales, a report by the law reform organisation JUSTICE called for fundamental change to the way in which hearings operate (Marks, 2016). The report redefined the concept of courts and tribunals as flexible spaces and urged greater use of technology; the authors identified an opportunity to be seized. The HMCTS courts modernisation programme, falling behind and with overrunning costs (National Audit Office, 2018), has not yet seized that opportunity. However, for the first time, there was a pilot of 'video hearings' in the tax tribunal, where appellants and representatives from the tax office attended remotely from their home or office. It was independently evaluated by Rossner and Tait (2020): '[P]articipants were able to access their hearings easily, understood the proceedings and considered the format to be appropriately formal. This was despite the fact they experienced frequent technical disruptions.'

The implications of the modernisation reforms that HMCTS has been pursuing, especially in the criminal courts, have given rise to many concerns about remote attendance (Gibbs, 2017; Padfield and Hawker, 2017) and the need for 'significant investment' to improve court audio-video equipment (Fielding et al, 2020:11). Remote hearings may never be appropriate for some court users, according to the interim findings of an Equality and Human Rights Commission study into vulnerable defendants in the criminal justice system: 'Most of our evidence focused on the barriers that video hearings can present to defendants with a cognitive impairment, mental health condition and/ or neuro-diverse condition. We found that for many people with these impairments, a video hearing would not be suitable' (EHRC, 2020: 10).

However, the concerns raised about the reforms go much wider than this. The House of Commons Justice Committee (2019) sounded alarm bells:

> Courts service modernisation, including use of better IT to be more efficient, is long- overdue. But we have found that poor digital skills, limited access to technology and low levels of literacy and legal knowledge raise barriers against access to new services provided by digital means ... We received powerful evidence of a court system in administrative chaos, with serious staff shortages threatening to compromise the fairness of proceedings. (Para 149)

Then, in the spring of 2020, an already stressed court system was forced to make sudden, radical changes to the way in which hearings are conducted and thus how court users participate.

Court reform, the COVID-19 pandemic and court user participation

On 23 March 2020, the Prime Minister announced strict curbs on travel and social contact in order to prevent the transmission of COVID-19 (BBC, 2020b). It does not appear that the courts in England and Wales could immediately turn to a pre-set pandemic response plan 'to ensure the continuity of vital court operations' (Task Force on Pandemic Preparedness Planning for the Courts, 2007: 3) with, for example, provisions to facilitate press and public access to remote hearings (Task Force on Pandemic Preparedness Planning for the Courts, 2007). In England and Wales, the decision was taken to keep open some 'priority courts' (MoJ, 2020), while the majority closed to lawyers and the public. Overnight, the centuries-old presumption in favour of face-to-face hearings was replaced with a presumption in favour of hearings facilitated by technology so that participants could join in from separate locations ('remote hearings'). This was a very rapid and unanticipated acceleration of a trend that was already in progress, under the courts modernisation programme.

The approach was, 'where it can be safely done and without risks to the integrity of the legal process, the wheels of justice should keep turning at their pre-crisis rate'.[13] HMCTS, the Ministry of Justice and the judiciary necessarily worked fast and hard to produce extensive guidance for judges and lawyers involved in remote hearings. There were pressing practical issues such as which video platform to use and how to prepare electronic bundles of documents for hearings.

Judges were given the discretion to determine how the remote hearing would replace the traditional face-to-face, oral hearing in court: for example, by telephone (*Anwer* v *Central Bridging Loans Ltd* [2020] EWHC 765 (Ch)), by video (*A Clinical Commissioning Group* v *AF and Others* [2020] EWCOP 16), by a combination of telephone and video (*Kavaarupo* v *Nursing and Midwifery Council* [2020] EWHC 731 (Admin)) or by evidence and submission in writing (*Gil* v *London Borough of Camden* [2020] EWHC 735 (QB)).

It rapidly became clear that practitioners and court users could have very different experiences (Kitzinger, 2020), resulting in 'a gulf between lawyers and lay parties' perspectives' (Jaganmohan, 2020). One barrister and sometime tribunal chair summed up the position as follows:

> The fact that some lawyers or participants would rather engage in conventional, in-person, hearings does not

mean that one held remotely has not been fair. Certainly, there are different dynamics, particularly around the human inter-reaction between witness and questioner and between advocate and tribunal. But whether that materially alters the instinctive assessments that are a feature of the conventional process and, if it does, whether one loses anything that is truly useful and reliable is open to question. (Norris, 2020)

Despite a steady stream of new guidance for lawyers,[14] advice for court users was exceedingly brief and of limited value since it came with no explanation of what it means to 'participate effectively' or what 'adjustments' to a remote hearing might be possible:

> Audio and video hearings provide an additional channel for conducting a hearing and should be as accessible as possible. But they may not be suitable for everyone. Please tell the court or tribunal if there are any circumstances about yourself or your case which may affect or impair your ability to participate effectively in an audio or video hearing. This will inform the judiciary's decision. Reasonable adjustments will be made. (HMCTS, 2020)

HMCTS had rightly identified the issue of participation for court users, but without providing practical guidance. It is suggested that placing effective participation at the heart of the design of practical guidance for court users would be a good place to start. Using our empirical findings, and in particular the *Ten Points of Participation* (see Chapter Three generally and Box 3.1 in particular), we have suggested what the guidance might cover in Table 5.2.

Use of the *Ten Points of Participation* to frame guidance for court users is one example of their application. The *Ten Points of Participation* can also help practitioners to reflect on their

Table 5.2: Ten Points of Participation as a provisional framework for court user guidance

	Participation entails:	Guidance might cover:
1	The provision and/or elicitation of information for the court	The way the court user can provide information (including evidence) and how the court will provide it to the user
2	Being informed about proceedings	Sources of information about how the hearing works and sources of advice on use of accessible language without reliance on legal jargon
3	Having legal representation	Sources of legal representation and information about funding so that participants may consider representation and understand that it is intended as a facilitator of, not a substitute for, their participation
4	Protection of well-being	Adaptations (including but not limited to special measures) and how they may be sought and applied according to the needs of the court user and the case
5	The 'management' of the court user, such that disruption to proceedings is minimised	The court user's responsibilities and potential consequences (for the individual and the court process) of disruption
6	Presence at proceedings	Implications of virtual versus physical presence, and the bases on which informed choices might be made (where applicable) about whether, and how, to attend proceedings
	Functions of participation:	**Guidance might cover:**
7	The exercise of legal rights	What legal rights are and how they differ depending on the type of court user and court

(continued)

Table 5.2: Ten Points of Participation as a provisional framework for court user guidance (continued)

8	Enabling court decision making	How the court user's participation can facilitate decision making
9	Legitimation of court processes and outcomes	How having a 'voice' in proceedings can contribute to perceptions of the fairness of the process and outcome
10	Potential therapeutic benefits	Potential benefits to the individual, separate from the legal outcome, that may arise from participation

own understandings of participation and thus their approach to court users before, during and after a hearing. For example,

- Which aspects of participation, if any, do they regard as most important, and do they regard any as unimportant?
- Do they explicitly discuss with court users the court's expectations of their participation, and how it contributes to the overall process?

Court user participation is also a necessary consideration when guidance for practitioners is produced. Note, for example, that advocates' robes – worn in the courtroom for some hearings – have been dispensed with for COVID-19 remote hearings:

- 'Advocates are not required to wear Robes for any hearing. Smart business wear is, however, appropriate for hearings where the advocate(s) can be seen' (Godsmark, 2020: para 18).
- 'Dress professionally, but not in robes unless specifically asked to do so and appear as if attending the court or tribunal in person' (ICCA, 2020: 6).

Is this decision to dispense with robes because advocates might not have access to their robes? Perhaps it is to prevent advocates feeling awkward joining a remote video hearing in robes from home? It may have been a practitioner-centric decision; however, from the perspective of court user participation, the judge and advocates wearing 'robes' might have particular advantages in remote hearings. It might assist court users to see at a glance who is who. (In a traditional courtroom, the physical location of the judge and advocates usually indicates their role and position in the power hierarchy, but that is lost on a standard video conferencing platform.) Robes, or even just gowns (rather than wigs and gowns), could add legitimacy to a remote hearing. Robes might also add weight to judicial attempts to manage disruptive participants, something that is particularly relevant when judges report a 'growing problem of participants not respecting the reality that although they were not physically present in a court room, they were taking part in court proceedings with all the constraints on behaviour that implies' (Burnett et al, 2020).

Urgent changes to court procedures have given rise to rapid preliminary research, including a consultation at the request of the President of the Family Division (Ryan et al, 2020). In *B (Children) (Remote Hearing: Interim Care Order)* [2020] EWCA Civ 584, the President noted 'a qualitative difference between a remote hearing conducted over the telephone and one undertaken via a video platform'. There is, of course, also a qualitative difference between participating remotely and participating in a court or tribunal room. Emergency measures will give judges and practitioners first-hand experience of some of the challenges of participating remotely and, perhaps, new insights into the challenges already faced by vulnerable witnesses participating remotely under special measures provisions.

Conclusion

Participation by lay court users in oral hearings is deemed by law to be essential to the delivery of justice. However, what precisely is meant by participation, and its functions, are not clearly or consistently defined. Ongoing policy and practice reforms variously support and undermine participation – for example:

- On the 'support' side are the increasing provision for vulnerable court users; growing efforts to make court proceedings more comprehensible generally; and (arguably) greater efficiency or speed of proceedings.
- Factors on the 'undermine' side may include legal aid cuts; court closures and associated use of remote methods of attending court; and loss of 'local justice'.

Practitioners recognise the importance of participation and of their own role in supporting it, although they vary in how exactly they understand the term. Practitioners also do much to support participation in practice; however, the findings of this study should encourage them to remain vigilant about the barriers to participation and to keep under review the extent to which it is achieved in practice.[15] It is clear that participation can be severely constrained by multiple factors, including the wide disparities between court users' social worlds and the formal world of the courtroom.

There was already an accelerating trend towards replacement of physical attendance at court with remote methods – including online pleas in the criminal courts, online cases in civil courts, attendance by video–link in criminal and other courts, and the potential development of entirely virtual hearings. There were two contrasting rationales supporting this trend: protection of the vulnerable, as well as cost and efficiency savings, under the umbrella of the wider court reform. The past few years have also seen many practitioners, academics and other commentators raise significant concerns about remote court hearings and remote attendance and about the implications for participation by court users, access to justice and open justice. There has been little research or analysis which has addressed these concerns in a thorough or systematic way.

The COVID-19 pandemic has been a major impetus for rapidly expanded use of alternatives to face-to-face court attendance and hearings, at least temporarily and potentially over the medium to longer term. At a minimum, it compels us to reflect on the implications for remote participation at court hearings, and to challenge some assumptions about these developments. Questions that are raised include:

- Does wider use of remote court hearings provide opportunities to overcome barriers to participation – for example, excessive formality and complexity?
- Are there circumstances, or parts of the justice system, in which remote attendance must always be avoided and, if so, why and how?
- How can learning about good and poor practice and procedures be compiled and shared – both nationally and internationally?

There is no doubt that COVID-19 has acted as an accelerant to the HMCTS court reform programme. Which reforms introduced under the emergency measures stand the test of time when the immediate health crisis has past remains to be seen. It is possible that the challenges of participating in virtual hearings will fuel support for a return to face-to-face hearings, at least until there is further research, better technology and more detailed planning of virtual hearings.

Aspirations for research, policy and practice

For hundreds of years, the traditional approach to hearings in England and Wales has been one in which participants are co-located and communicating face-to-face. Exceptions to the traditional means of participation in court have been made for those who are distressed, young, incapacitated or unable to attend court because they are physically unwell or overseas. Internationally, innovative ideas to promote participation have been shared, imported and adapted. These initiatives have been relatively slow to take root in new jurisdictions and remain under-researched, niche, temporary 'fixes'. For the vast majority of court users, the 'usual way' of participating has meant face-to-face in court. Barriers to participation exist for the majority of court users: these arise, for example, from the complexity of the law and the language of the courtroom; the emotional price of being in a hearing about conflict, loss and disadvantage; and the often wide social, cultural and educational disparities between most court practitioners and most court users as individuals.

When the emergency measures were introduced to tackle the spread of the COVID-19 virus, the new experimental way of participating in a court hearing was remotely. The advice for practitioners soon became legion, but the advice for court users was minimal; it promised 'reasonable adjustments' for 'effective participation' in remote hearings without saying what these meant.

Case law[16] and policy, while referring to effective participation, are largely silent on the form that participation should take or its functions. This study now offers a framework – albeit a preliminary one because further research is required with court users. It is intended that this framework, based on the *Ten Points of Participation*, should guide policy- and practice-oriented engagement with witnesses and parties so that they might better understand what to expect in court and what is expected of them. It should also form the basis of much-needed future research involving court users.

Looking ahead, justice researchers and policy makers around the world have a key role to play in placing court user participation at the heart of court reform through:

- engagement with court users to better understand from their perspective what it means to *participate effectively*;
- coordinated, international, cross-jurisdictional information sharing about issues affecting court user participation;
- research into new, creative approaches that extend beyond remote hearings which simply emulate a traditional hearing.

The mid- to long-term implications of COVID-19 are unknown, although inevitably public funding, including for justice, will be severely tested. Some practitioners may favour a return to 'traditional' hearings (if that is even possible), while others may hope that remote hearings become the 'new normal'. Research shows that 'traditional' hearings can be marginalising and disempowering for court users; however, remote hearings, if poorly configured, might retain the old barriers to participation and add new ones. Whatever direction court reform takes, it requires a new approach based on a better understanding of 'effective participation'. For this to happen, it is the responsibility of researchers and policy makers, as well as those who work in the courts and tribunals, to place the participation of *all* court users at the heart of permanent court reform.

Notes

[1] Fortuitously, for other professional reasons not funded by this project, the author of this chapter visited Australia, Belize, Chile, Northern Ireland, Scotland and the US as an invited conference speaker during the course of this project, where practitioners and judges readily shared examples of adaptations in courtrooms in their jurisdictions. Thanks are due to the following organisations which facilitated the author's visits/ research in the field in jurisdictions outside England and Wales: ACT Human Rights Commission, Caribbean Association of Judicial Officers, Department of Justice, Northern Ireland, Foreign and Commonwealth Office, Fundación Amparo y Justicia (Chile), Judicial Institute for Scotland, Law Society of Scotland, New South Wales Department of Communities and Justice, New South Wales Police Department and NSW Ombudsman.

2   Initial search term in September 2017: '(witness or victim or defendant or party) AND (vulnerab★ or intimidated or young or child or disab★) AND (special measure★ or adjust★ or adapt★) AND (in court or trial) AND (innovat★ or reform★)'.

3   Adolescents are defined as those who are between 14 and 18 years of age.

4   Source: private correspondence between the author and intermediaries and judges.

5   The concept of the ground rules hearings was devised and developed by the author in the course of intermediary training from 2003 onwards and subsequent research about intermediary practice in England and Wales.

6   Decided: 26 September 2013. Full judgment available from: http://caselaw.findlaw.com/wa-supreme-court/1645704.html

7   Email correspondence between the author and the Director of the Bocalan Trust, Chile.

8   2016 BCSC 1680.

9   Information provided by email to the author from the intermediary in the case.

10   Information provided to the author in a meeting with the judge in the case.

11   Email correspondence (27 September 2017 and 3 October 2017) and meeting with Dr Spruin.

12   'The best time to plant a tree was 20 years ago. The second best time is now.'

13   Judge Daniel Alexander QC in *Heineken Supply Chain BV v Anheuser-Busch Inbev SA (Rev 1)* [2020] EWHC 892 (Pat), para 28.

14   At the time of writing, in total 84 new COVID-19 remote hearing guidance documents were on the HMCTS website. They had been gradually uploaded between 23 March and 17 April 2020, with some general in nature and others applicable to specific courts or tribunals. See www.judiciary.uk/coronavirus-covid-19-advice-and-guidance/

15   This accords with the recommendation in the JUSTICE report on *Understanding Courts* that 'There should be an expressly stated overriding objective – across all jurisdictions – that professionals should have as a primary consideration the effective participation of lay users. In other words, that the professionals adapt proceedings to ensure lay users comprehend the process' (JUSTICE, 2019: 108).

16   For example, see *R* v *Thomas* [2020] EWCA Crim 117.

References

BBC (2020a) Law in Action, 'Supporting evidence', 5 March, available from: www.bbc.co.uk/programmes/m000fvvp

BBC (2020b) 'Coronavirus: strict new curbs on life in UK announced by PM', 24 March, available from: www.bbc.co.uk/news/uk-52012432

Burd, K.A. and Mcquiston, D.E. (2019) 'Facility dogs in the courtroom: comfort without prejudice?', *Criminal Justice Review*, 44(4), 1–22.

Burnett, I., Etherton, T. and McFarlane, A. (2020) 'Message for Circuit and District Judges sitting in Civil and Family from the Lord Chief Justice, Master of the Rolls and President of the Family Division', 9 April, available from: www.judiciary.uk/wp-content/uploads/2020/04/Message-to-CJJ-and-DJJ-9-April-2020.pdf

Colorado Judicial Department (2004) 'Access to the courts: a resource guide to providing reasonable accommodations for people with disabilities for judicial officers, probation and court staff', available from: www.thearc.org/file/ADAresourceguide.pdf

Cooper, P., Backen, P. and Marchant, R. (2015) 'Getting to grips with ground rules hearings – a checklist for judges, advocates and intermediaries', *Criminal Law Review*, 6: 420–35.

Cooper, P. and Mattison, M. (2017) 'Intermediaries, vulnerable people and the quality of evidence: an international comparison of three versions of the English intermediary model', *International Journal of Evidence and Proof*, 21(4): 351–70.

Cooper, P. and Mattison, M. (2018) 'Section 28 pre-recorded cross-examination: what is in store for advocates in 2018', *Criminal Law and Justice Weekly*, 182: 7–9.

Corish, S. (2015) 'Issues for the defence in trials with pre-recording of the evidence of vulnerable witnesses', *Criminal Law Journal*, 39: 187–97.

Courthouse Dogs Foundation (2020) 'Where dogs are working', available from: https://courthousedogs.org/dogs/where/where-united-states/

Delhi High Court (nd) 'Guidelines for recording of evidence of vulnerable witnesses in criminal matters', available from: http://delhihighcourt.nic.in/writereaddata/upload/Notification/NotificationFile_LCWCD2X4.PDF

Donaldson, K.M. (2017) 'Defense and prosecuting attorney perceptions of facility dogs in the courtroom', Walden University, doctoral dissertation, available from: http://scholarworks.waldenu.edu/cgi/viewcontent.cgi?article=5042&context=dissertations

The Equalities and Human Rights Commission (2020) 'Inclusive justice: a system designed for all – interim evidence report – video hearings and their impact on effective participation', available from: www.equalityhumanrights.com/sites/default/files/inclusive_justice_a_system_designed_for_all_interim_report_0.pdf

Fielding, N., Braun, S., Hieke, G. and Mainwaring, C. (2020) 'Video enabled justice evaluation', Sussex Police and Crime Commissioner and University of Surrey, available from: http://spccweb.thco.co.uk/media/4851/vej-final-report-ver-11b.pdf

Gallagher, C. (2016) '"At the moment, court is a very frightening place for a child" – young victims in Ireland's legal system', *The Journal*, 24 May, available from: www.thejournal.ie/child-court-protection-2784424-May2016/

Gibbs, P. (2017) *Defendants on Video: Conveyor Belt Justice or a Revolution in Access?*, London: Transform Justice.

Glazer, M. (2018) 'Assessing the perceptions of the use of a courthouse facility dog program with child and youth witnesses', Electronic Thesis and Dissertation Repository, 5265, available from: https://ir.lib.uwo.ca/etd/5265

Godsmark, N. (2020) 'COVID-19 Nottinghamshire, Derbyshire, Lincolnshire Protocol', 10 April, available from: www.civillitigationbrief.com/2020/04/14/covid-19-nottinghamshire-derbyshire-lincolnshire-protocol-hhj-godsmark-qc-designated-civil-judge/

Gómez, S.E., updated by Fernández-Acevedo, F.J. and Depolo, R. (2010) 'Update: essential issues of the Chilean legal system', Hauser Global Law School Program, available from: www.nyulawglobal.org/globalex/Chile1.html#_Regarding_the_Criminal_Procedure%20Re

Grant, M. (2014) 'Hawk, Calgary police dog, to help child witnesses in sex abuse case', 29 October, available from: www.cbc.ca/news/canada/calgary/hawk-calgary-police-dog-to-help-child-witnesses-in-sex-abuse-case-1.2817476

Grimm, A.L. (2013) 'An examination of why permitting therapy dogs to assist child-victims when testifying during criminal trials should not be permitted', *Journal of Gender, Race and Justice*, 16(1): 263–92.

Hanna, K., Davies, E., Henderson, E., Crothers, C. and Rotherham, C. (2010) *Child Witnesses in the New Zealand Criminal Courts: A Review of Practice and Implications for Policy*, New Zealand: New Zealand Law Foundation.

Her Majesty's Courts and Tribunals Service (2020) 'HMCTS telephone and video hearings during coronavirus outbreak', 18 March, available from: www.gov.uk/guidance/hmcts-telephone-and-video-hearings-during-coronavirus-outbreak#court-and-tribunal-users

Holder, C. (2013) 'All dogs go to court: the impact of court facility dogs as comfort for child witnesses on a defendant's right to a fair trial', *Houston Law Review*, 50: 1155–88.

House of Commons Justice Committee (2019) 'Court and tribunal reforms', HC 190, 31 October, p 3, available from: https://publications.parliament.uk/pa/cm201919/cmselect/cmjust/190/190.pdf

Howard, K., McCann, C. and Dudley, M. (2019) ' "It's really good … why hasn't it happened earlier?" Professionals' perspectives on the benefits of communication assistance in the New Zealand youth justice system', *Australian and New Zealand Journal of Criminology*, 1–20.

Inns of Court College of Advocacy (2020) 'Principles for remote advocacy', Version 2, 16 April, available from: www.icca.ac.uk/wp-content/uploads/2020/04/Principles-for-Remote-Advocacy-version-2.pdf

Jaganmohan, M. (2020) 'Remote hearings: a gulf between lawyers and lay parties?', The Transparency Project, 29 March, available from: www.transparencyproject.org.uk/remote-hearings-a-gulf-between-lawyers-and-lay-parties/

Jonker, G. and Swanzen, R. (2007) 'Intermediary services for child witnesses testifying in South African criminal courts', *SUR International Journal of Human Rights*, 6(4), 91–113.

Judicial Education Institute of Trinidad and Tobago (2015) *Criminal Bench Book*, available from: www.ttlawcourts.org/jeibooks/books/ttcriminalbenchbook.pdf

Judicial Education Institute of Trinidad and Tobago (2018) 'Justice through a gender lens: gender equality protocol for judicial officers', available from: www.ttlawcourts.org/jeibooks/books/geptt.pdf

JUSTICE (2019) *Understanding Courts: A Report by JUSTICE*, London: JUSTICE.

Kitzinger, C. (2020) 'Remote justice: a family perspective', The Transparency Project, 29 March, available from: www.transparencyproject.org.uk/remote-justice-a-family-perspective/

Marks, A. (2016) 'What is a court? A report by JUSTICE', available from: https://justice.org.uk/wp-content/uploads/2016/05/JUSTICE-What-is-a-Court-Report-2016.pdf

Ministry of Justice (2020) 'COVID-19 stakeholder update', email to stakeholders, 31 March.

Morrison, J. (2019) 'The dog helped them find their words', Churchill Fellow Report, available from: www.churchilltrust.com.au/fellows/detail/4336/Julie+Morrison

Mosqueda, L. (2012) 'Elder abuse pocket reference: a medical/legal resource for California judicial officers', San Francisco: Judicial Council of California, available from: www.courts.ca.gov/documents/ElderAbusePDoc.pdf

National Audit Office (2018) *HM Courts and Tribunals Service: Early Progress in Transforming Courts and Tribunals*, London: NAO.

National Crime Victim Law Institute (2013) 'Facility dogs: Helping victims access justice and exercise their rights', NCVLI Victim Law Bulletin, available from: https://law.lclark.edu/live/files/21750-facility-dogshelping-victims-access-justice-and

Norris, W. (2020) 'Remote hearings; here to stay or just while needs must?', 16 April, 39 Essex Chambers, available from: www.39essex.com/remote-hearings-here-to-stay-or-just-while-needs-must/

O'Leary, C. and Feely, M. (2018) 'Alignment of the Irish legal system and Article 13.1 of the CRPD for witnesses with communication difficulties', Disability Studies Quarterly, available from: https://dsq-sds.org/article/view/5587/4887

Padfield, N. and Hawker, T. (2017) 'Editorial: sentencing via video link', Criminal Law Review, 8: 585–6.

Parliament South Australia (2020) Hansard, Grievance Debate: Communication Partner Service, 5 February, House of Assembly, available from: http://hansardpublic.parliament.sa.gov.au/Pages/HansardResult.aspx#/docid/HANSARD-11-37075

Rossner, M. and Tait, D. (2020) 'Courts are moving to video during coronavirus, but research shows it's hard to get a fair trial remotely', The Conversation, available from: https://theconversation.com/courts-are-moving-to-video-during-coronavirus-but-research-shows-its-hard-to-get-a-fair-trial-remotely-134386

Ryan, M., Harker, L. and Rothera, S. (2020) 'Resource: remote hearings in the family justice system: a rapid consultation', Nuffield Family Justice Observatory, May, available from: www.nuffieldfjo.org.uk/resource/remote-hearings-rapid-consultation

Scottish Court Service (2015) 'Evidence and procedure review report', March, Edinburgh: Scottish Court Service, available from: www.scotcourts.gov.uk/docs/default-source/aboutscs/reports-and-data/reports-data/evidence-and-procedure-full-report---publication-version-pdf.pdf?sfvrsn=2

Scottish Courts and Tribunal Service (2019) 'New evidence and hearings suite for children and vulnerable witnesses opens', 18 November, Scottish Courts and Tribunal Service, available from: www.scotcourts.gov.uk/about-the-scottish-court-service/scs-news/2019/11/18/new-evidence-and-hearings-suite-for-children-and-vulnerable-witnesses-opens

Shukla, R. (2018) 'Vulnerable witnesses and criminal justice system: role of intermediaries', 30 June, available from: www.livelaw.in/vulnerable-witnesses-and-criminal-justice-system-role-of-intermediaries/

Spencer, J.R. and Flin, R.H. (1990) The Evidence of Children: The Law and Psychology, London: Blackstone Press.

Spruin, E., Dempster, T. and Mozova, K. (2020) 'Facility dogs as a tool for building rapport and credibility with child witnesses', International Journal of Law Crime and Justice.

Spruin, E. and Mozova, K. (2017) 'Using specially trained dogs in the Criminal Justice System', British Psychological Society, Special Edition: Reviews of Presentations, and Symposia at the DFP Annual Conference 2017, ISSN: 2050–7348, Forensic Update 125, September, pp 30–41.

Sriram, J. (2017) 'The teddy bear courts: Goa's pioneering children's courtroom', 30 July, available from: www.vikalpsangam.org/article/the-teddy-bear-courts-goas-pioneering-childrens-courtroom/#.Xm5a3i2cY1I

Task Force on Pandemic Preparedness Planning for the Courts (2007) 'Guidelines for pandemic emergency preparedness planning: a road map for courts', March, American University Washington, DC and Bureau of Justice Assistance, available from: www.txcourts.gov/media/1353181/PandemicRoadMapFINAL-031407.pdf

Warnica, M. (2015) 'Zebra Centre support dog helps child witness testify', 6 March, available from: www.cbc.ca/news/canada/edmonton/zebra-centre-support-dog-helps-child-witness-testify-1.2984754

Wilcock, R., Crane, L., Hobson, Z., Nash, G., Kirke-Smith, M. and Henry, L.A. (2018) 'Supporting child witnesses during identification lineups: exploring the effectiveness of registered intermediaries', Applied Cognitive Psychology, 32(3): 367–75.

Index

References to figures, tables and boxes are in *italics*. Page numbers followed by 'n' refer to notes.

W

Y